LEARN TO
DRAW

10-WEEK COURSE
FOR ASPIRING ARTISTS

Barrington Barber

ARCTURUS

ARCTURUS

This edition published in 2022 by Arcturus Publishing Limited
26/27 Bickels Yard, 151–153 Bermondsey Street,
London SE1 3HA

ISBN: 978-1-78428-360-5
AD004938UK

Printed in China

Contents

Introduction

Drawing isn't a mystery – even if you haven't touched a drawing implement since childhood, you can start to draw now and achieve impressive results. In this book, you will find everything you need to develop your drawing skills, from the first basic exercises that are suitable for complete beginners, to more complex projects which involve looking at a subject in depth. I have given suggestions for 10 weeks of drawing practice, incorporating time-honoured methods used by art students and professional artists. Even if you are a practised artist, I encourage you to follow the course from the beginning as drawing exercises are always valuable to your development. In the first sections, we will look at how to manipulate line, texture and shading to make recognizable forms with a degree of dimensionality. Then we will consolidate those skills across a full range of subject matter, from objects around the house to plants, animals, landscapes and people. As the course progresses, you will revisit certain subject areas, exploring them in more depth and looking at how to create detailed finished drawings.

When you have completed the exercises in this book, you should see a marked progress in your drawing skills, whatever your starting point. Don't worry if you have to miss a week or if you don't finish all the exercises within exactly seven days; the main things are to practise as regularly as you can, to correct mistakes when you see them and above all to enjoy your drawing.

Materials

When you first start to draw the most obvious tools to use are pencils, as you will have used these since you were a child and will feel very comfortable with them. I suggest you start with B and 2B pencils, which have slightly softer leads than HB pencils. Later on in the course, when you are feeling more confident and preparing to take your drawing skills further, you could try a variety of mediums to see the different marks they make, enjoying the way you can expand your range of techniques. You will find drawing implements described in Week 6 (see pages 75–88), with exercises to try them out on.

For your surfaces, you will need medium-weight cartridge paper, which you can buy in sheets or in a sketchbook. The latter will be more versatile, because you can take it around with you as well as using it at home. The sizes you will find convenient for travelling with are A5, A4 and A3 – anything larger is unwieldy.

A drawing board to use at home can be bought ready-made from an art supplies shop, but it's easy enough to make one cheaply by sawing it from a piece of MDF or thick plywood; an A2 size is most useful. To attach your cartridge paper to the board, traditional clips or drawing pins can be used, but I prefer masking tape, which is light, easy to adjust and doesn't seem to damage the paper if it is used carefully.

Line, Shape and Texture

The exercises in this first week are primarily designed for people who haven't done very much drawing, but even if you are already quite practised you may find that following the examples shown here is a good way to loosen yourself up for the rest of the course. The main point of them is to work on the basic skills necessary to draw anything with some degree of verisimilitude. The practice of making marks, which after all is what drawing consists of, never loses its usefulness however accomplished you become.

So included in this section are exercises in drawing lines, tones, textures, and then simple shapes. All of the latter need a certain amount of control of the pencil, and practising this is never time wasted. You will also find exercises in simple perspective to introduce you to the practicalities of drawing shapes that appear to have some dimension.

These are followed by drawing the outlines of objects you have in front of you in order to familiarize yourself with working from life. This is where the real skill of an artist is honed, and it is something that you will never stop practising if you want to draw well. Finally, you will find exercises that give you some practice in adding texture to the objects that you draw in order to make them look more realistic.

Mark Making

These exercises are mainly for the benefit of complete beginners in drawing, but even if you are reasonably competent they will still be of great benefit. It is practising every day that produces manual dexterity, which is essentially what the artist needs. The more often you follow exercises such as these the more your hand and eye learn to work together, making your drawing more skilful.

Don't ignore the aesthetic quality of making marks; try to make your group of exercises look good on the paper.

Exercise 1

Start by making a scribbly line in all directions. Limit it to an area and try to produce a satisfying texture.

Next try short, staccato marks that fill the space. Notice how none of them overlap and the spaces in between remain similar.

When you are drawing these more controlled uniform lines, make them all the same length and the same distance apart, keeping them as straight as possible.

Now take a line for a walk, but don't cross over it anywhere. This may seem rather obsessive, but it is a step on the way to drawing recognizable forms.

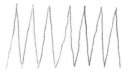

Next try a variety of straight lines, again trying to get them straight and the same distance apart, fitting into an imagined rectangle. First do diagonals from lower left to upper right, then horizontals, then diagonals from upper left to lower right. Next, try the two diagonals across each other to form a net, then the horizontals and verticals in the same fashion.

To practise more circular forms, make spirals. Work from outside to inside, clockwise and anti-clockwise, then tighter with the lines closer together; next work from the centre outwards, anti-clockwise then clockwise.

Now zigzag your pencil up and down.

Use the same action, but incorporate some loops.

Try to produce a dark mass with lines going up and down.

Next, lay another mass of lines horizontally over this dark mass.

Finally, add third and fourth layers both at diagonals.

Exercise 2

The next exploration in mark making is to draw a mass of zigzags in a continuous line crisscrossing over itself.

Now make softer, curvy lines overlapping themselves.

And now cloud-like shapes, going round and round in a continual line overlapping itself.

Next come circles, but not large – lots of them lined up both horizontally and vertically.

Inside each circle, put a nicely drawn spot.

Next make a network of vertical and horizontal lines, drawn very carefully.

Spread a mass of dots over an area as evenly as possible. Remember that this is training for the eye as well as the hand, so the evenness of the dots is important.

Draw several rows of small squares in lines as evenly as possible, as square as possible and lined up both vertically and horizontally.

This exercise is a bit harder to draw evenly, but try it anyway. Make rows of triangles fitting together so that the space between them is as even as possible and they are lined up horizontally and vertically.

Draw rows of spirals joined together as if they were the waves on the sea. Under them draw rows of waves, again as even as you can get them.

For the rest of the exercises on this page, the emphasis is on lightness of touch and control of the direction.

The first one is a vague circular shape of closely drawn lines, light in pressure to create an area of tone.

Using the same technique, draw horizontal lines.

Next, make them vertically.

Then draw them diagonally, slanting to the left.

Again working diagonally, start dark with some pressure, gradually lightening the touch until it fades away.

Now make a series of similar shaded areas, starting from a curved drawn line so that one edge is defined.

Shade away from a zigzag edge.

Then shade away from an S-curved edge.

Now draw a circle and shade inside and outside of opposite edges.

Finally, do the same again only with two circles, one within the other.

Basic Shapes

So far, the exercises you have done with your pencil have been a bit like doodling. The next phase is a rather more intellectual one, where you have to envisage a form in your mind before trying to draw it.

Exercise 1

First, without too much thought, draw a circle as perfectly as you can. Now close your eyes and see in your mind's eye a perfect circle. It is extraordinary how we can do this yet draw something much less than perfect.

For your second attempt, draw one very lightly with a compass and then go over it in freehand. With practice of this kind it won't be long before your freehand circles improve.

Now try an equilateral triangle – that is, a triangle that has all three sides equal in length. Not quite so easy as it looks, is it? But there is also a mechanical device to help you here: describe a circle with a compass, then draw the triangle within it, all angles touching the circle.

Next, a square. You will know that all the sides of a square are equal in length, and the corners are all right angles, but it can take a bit of time to get that right in the drawing.

Because you are not used to seeing it so much, it is not so easy to draw a square balanced up on one corner, like a diamond shape. You will find it harder to get the sides equal.

Now we move on to slightly more complex shapes. The point of this is to get your eye, brain and hand acting together, so that gradually the practice of drawing becomes easier.

First, draw a five-pointed star without lifting your pencil from the paper. This is also easier drawn inside a circle with all the angles touching it, but try it with and without.

Secondly, try a six-pointed star, which is merely two equilateral triangles superimposed on one another.

Thirdly, draw a star of eight points, which is one square superimposed on another.

Now try an egg-shape. This is narrower at one end than the other; draw it with the broader end at the base.

The crescent is another shape much harder than it looks at first glance, but the secret is to realize that the curve is a part of a circle. Try it freehand and then with a compass-drawn circle to help.

Exercise 2

In this exercise we start to look at ways of making things appear three-dimensional, in a conventional way – that is, they are only approximations of perspective, which is the way we tend to see shapes in space.

Draw a square, then another the same size but slightly above and to one side of the first. Join the corners with straight lines to link them up, giving a result like a transparent cube.

The next figure is similar, but put in only three of the joining lines so that the cube looks solid rather than transparent.

Now another way of drawing a cube; draw a flattened parallelogram, like a diamond on its side, and then project straight vertical lines down from the corners of this shape to another diamond shape below.

This time draw only three of the joining lines and two edges of the lower diamond, so that the cube looks solid again.

Next, draw a cylinder. First draw an ellipse – a flattened circle – then project two parallel lines vertically downwards to meet a similar ellipse.

Try again, only this time leave out the upper edge of the lower ellipse to make the cylinder look more solid.

Reverse the process so that the upper ellipse has only one edge; the cylinder now appears to be seen from below.

Now move on to cones, which are just two converging straight lines with an ellipse at the wider end.

Try this without part of the ellipse and then with the cone balanced on its point.

Exercise 3

You won't have found any of those exercises difficult after a bit of practice. The next stage is to practise making areas of tone on spheres, cubes, cylinders and cones.

First draw a circle as accurately as you can. Now, with very light strokes, put an area of tone over the left-hand half of the circle. Increase the intensity in a crescent shape around the lower left-hand side of the circle, leaving a slight area closest to the edge to act as the reflected light that you usually

get around the darker side of the sphere. Put in the cast shadow on the area that would be the ground, spilling out to the left and fading as it gets further from the sphere.

Now have a go at a cube, covering the left-hand side with a darkish tone. When this is dark enough, cover the other vertical side evenly all over with a much lighter tone. All that is needed then is a cast shadow as before, but fitting the squarer shape of the figure.

A cylinder is similar to a sphere, but the shading is only on the vertical surface. Again make a column of darker tone just away from the left-hand edge.

With a cone you have to allow for the narrowing shape, which is reflected in the cast shadow.

Simple Perspective

In order to draw in a way that gives an effect of three dimensions you will need to learn a little about perspective, which is a way to make depth and space look more convincing. In life, perspective gives us an ability to assess the placing of objects and people in relation to one another, and gives us a framework for constructing landscapes and interiors. We will be studying perspective in greater detail in Week 7 (pages 89–102).

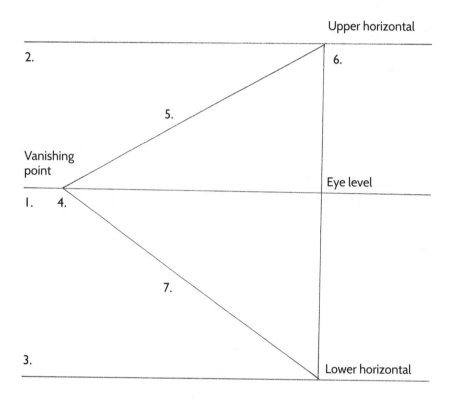

A **Step 1**

First, construct three horizontal lines that are parallel to each other across the page. The central one should be slightly nearer the top line than the bottom line. This central line (1) represents your eye level, which will always be the line of the horizon. The others are the upper horizontal (2) and the lower horizontal (3).

Now, to the right of the centre of your space, draw a vertical line from the upper horizontal to the lower horizontal (6). Fix a point on the eye-level line and join the two ends of the vertical line to this point, which is called the vanishing point (4). These two lines are the upper perspective line (5) and the lower perspective line (7). You now have a triangle connecting the three horizontals and the vertical.

8. 9.

> **Step 2**
Next draw two vertical lines parallel to the original vertical, one to the right (9) and one to the left (8), which will cut across the two lines going to the vanishing point.

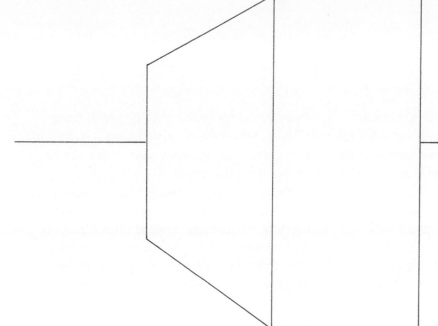

< **Step 3**
You can now rub out the construction lines to leave an apparent solid block such as a box or a building, with the horizon line across the back behind the object. This appears to give you a dimensional object in space which convinces the eye.

Drawing Objects

The exercises over the following pages should be fun, so try to feel at ease as you do them. Don't grip the pencil too tightly, keep your shoulders relaxed and don't hunch up or get too close to your work. Don't worry about mistakes – just correct them when you see them.

To do this next set of exercises you will need to have some simple household objects in front of you. I have chosen some items from my own house – yours don't have to be exactly the same, but it will help you to follow my drawings as well as having the actual object in front of you.

Before you start, look very carefully at each object to familiarize yourself with its shape. I have used glass objects for the first exercises, because you can see through them to understand how the shape works.

Exercise 1

My first object is a bottle, seen directly from the side. As it was exactly symmetrical, I put in a central line first. Then I drew an outline of its shape including the screw top, making sure that both sides were symmetrical.

From a higher eye level, I could see the bottle's rounded shape. To show this I needed to draw the elliptical shapes that circles make when seen from an oblique angle. Again I carefully constructed the shape on either side of a central vertical line.

The ellipses shown below the bottles demonstrate how they become flattened to a greater or lesser degree depending upon the eye level from which a rounded object is seen. Although they become deeper across the vertical axis the further they are below your eye level, the horizontal axis remains the same width.

Don't be put off by the difficulty of drawing ellipses, because even professional artists don't find them so easy; with practice, you will be able to draw them well.

The next object is a glass tumbler with some water in it – slightly easier to draw than the bottle because it has straight sides. Draw the outline first at eye level and then seen from slightly above. In the latter drawing there are three ellipses: the top edge of the glass, the surface of the water and the bottom of the glass.

The third object, a wine glass with some liquid in it, is a bit harder. Here you will see that there are three ellipses of varying width, but the object is still symmetrical from side to side. Go carefully and enjoy discovering the exact shape.

Exercise 2

Now you're ready to move on to a series of objects which are of varying difficulty. The drawing of the hammer is quite easy from the exact side view but is a bit trickier from a more oblique view.

There are two ways to draw the spoon, from the exact front and from the exact side, before you try a more natural view.

The pot is not too difficult if you have completed the rounded objects on page 12. The hardest part to draw accurately will be the double ellipse of the rim and lid.

The box is very simple – but beware of the third version, a slightly more complex view where the perspective can easily go wrong.

The teapot has a characteristic handle shape and rounded spout to get to grips with, but by now you are getting used to the problems of drawing like this. This sequence of objects is merely to give you practice in drawing, doing as many as you can in the time you have available.

The chair is more complex than it looks at first glance. Follow the same course of drawing it from the exact side and front before trying to draw it in perspective. Understanding the construction of the chair is useful when you are trying to draw it.

Shading Objects

All these objects are simple enough in outline. However, to make them look more three-dimensional and substantial, shading of some sort is needed.

Make line drawings of the objects as accurately as possible before starting to add the shading. On the book, shading to show the curve of the spine and fine lines giving an effect of the packed pages is almost all there is to do, with the addition of a small cast shadow to anchor it to a surface.

The pot needs quite heavy tone in the interior space to give some idea of the inner hollow. Then add a graduated tone around the cylinder and a small cast shadow to complete the picture.

The apple needs to be shaded in a vertical direction between the upper surface and the bottom, concentrating on the left-hand side to indicate the direction of the light. Also add a cast shadow and some shading where the stalk comes out of its hollow.

Textures and Materiality

Here we look at developing a feel for different types of materials and transferring their textural qualities on to paper. As in the first exercises on pages 6–7, take care over the appearance of your drawings as a group.

Grass

The first of these drawings of texture shows an impression of an area of grass-like tufts – that is to say, stylized patterns that resemble grass, not drawings taken directly from life. When you have done this version, you could try to draw a real lawn.

Wood

Now try doing this wooden plank, with its knots and wavy lines of growth. The floorboards in your house might be a good example of this kind of wood pattern.

Fur

This resembles fur, such as on a rug or the back of a cat. The short, wavy lines go in several directions, but follow a sort of pattern.

Water

This watery texture is achieved by keeping all the marks you make horizontal and joined together to create the effect of ripples. Smudge a little of the drawing to create greyer tones, but leave some untouched areas to look like reflected light.

Leaves

All that is needed to give the effect of thick, hedge-like leaves is a large number of small leaves drawn adjacent to and overlapping each other. Try to maintain a certain amount of variety in the angles of the leaves to make them more convincing.

Beach

Next, a drawing that resembles a pebbled beach, with countless stones of various sizes. Again, after drawing a conventional version like this, you could try working with a real area of pebbles or stones.

Clouds

This smoky texture is produced by using a soft pencil, then a paper stump to smudge the dark areas. After that, a little rubbing of some of the darker parts gives a cloudy look.

Drapery

This drapery is done by drawing descending curves to emulate cloth, and then using a paper stump to smudge and soften the edges of the tone. The only sharp lines should be at the sides where the cloth appears to be gathered up.

Practising Texture

Exercise 1

In the next two exercises we go a stage further with textures, exploring a girl's long curly hair and some fabric. To start with, draw a very careful but simple outline of the shapes of the cascading hair, getting a feeling of the way it winds and curves as it grows away from the head. It doesn't matter if you don't get some of the waves of hair quite right, as long as the main shapes are followed.

Having got the main shapes of the hair you can now build up a texture of lines and tone to produce a convincing impression. The hair can be worked in with strokes following the main shapes of the curves, in some cases drawn heavier and darker and elsewhere drawn much lighter and fainter. This gradually produces the look of hair in waves. Notice how often at the edges of the mass of hair the tone looks darker, and how there is a contrast between the dark under curve and the lighter upper curve where the larger waves curl round.

Exercise 2

With the fabric, first notice the main folds and carefully draw them in as accurately as you can. The texture here is much simpler to draw than hair, just needing either darker or lighter tones to indicate the folds. As this particular piece of fabric is an old sweater, it can be drawn softly and slightly rough in texture to indicate the look of wool.

Now for two more kinds of texture and materiality –
a basket and a plant. As before, draw in the main shapes
of the objects first, being careful to get some idea of how
the woven strands in the basket weave in and out of each
other, and the delicacy of the outline of the leaves.

Exercise 3

In the case of the basket, the difficulty is to achieve
the effect of the interweaving strands without drawing
every one exactly. Try to obtain a
general impression with the
lined-up marks so that the
weaving appears uniform
enough without looking too
clean-cut. Make sure that the
shaded parts are strong enough to
convince the eye of the depth of the
space inside and around the object.
Try not to overdraw on the lighter
areas so that the contrast between the
two parts will work better for you.

Exercise 4

With the plant, again the trick is to not overdraw the
darker areas. One or two of the leaves at the back and
bottom of the plant will be in deep shade, but most of
them will be relatively light in tone. Try not to make
your marks too heavy, because the plant has a rather
delicate nature. Again it doesn't matter too much if
some of your leaves are not exactly in the right place,
as long as they look fairly natural.

By the end of this first week you will have tackled a
large number of basic elements in the art of drawing.
This is an excellent achievement, and if you are
in the least unsure of your skill, you can
repeat these exercises whenever you like
to give yourself more confidence. That
goes for all the exercises in this book –
you can always hark back to an earlier
stage if things aren't working as
they should.

WEEK 2 Form and Tone

This week's exercises are all about trying to make the shape of the objects you draw look more realistic by establishing their form in more detail. In order to do this you will also have to keep working on your drawing of outline shapes and build further on what you have already begun to learn about tone. So, starting off with carefully drawn shapes, you need to follow this up with adding tone and shading to the forms to give a feeling of solidity. This needs quite a lot of practice, so there are many variations in the objects I have given you to draw. You will also begin to see how the methods that you use in one drawing can easily be adapted for other things that at first glance seem very different. The more you can practise these methods the better you will become at drawing.

One thing you will come to realize is that there is no such thing as a difficult or easy drawing; they all have the same degree of difficulty, although some may take longer because there is more complexity in the shape. Drawing only becomes easier with increased skill, and then of course you draw more extensively so the challenges also increase. One of the great things about art is that you never come to the point where you know it all – there is always further to go.

Developing Form and Tone

To start our investigations into developing form, we look at two objects, a thermos flask and a tumbler, made of metal and glass respectively. Whereas the flask needs a building-up of tone to show its rounded form and the darker parts of the metal, the glass tumbler needs only minimal shading, because it is transparent.

First just draw the outline shapes of the objects and in the vacuum flask mark where the edges of the brightest and darkest areas of tone are to be. In the glass tumbler just put in the edge shapes of the moulded glass and the surface of the water.

Having done this, put in all the darkest tones on the flask as smoothly as you can. Gradually fill up all the other areas where the tones are less intense, making sure that you leave the brightest bits as totally white, clean paper. When you have covered all the areas of tone, study the whole drawing to see if you need to strengthen any of the darkest parts.

With the glass tumbler the trick is not to do too much shading. Put in the very darkest parts first, noticing that there are not very many of them. Then add the medium and lightest tones, underdoing the tone rather than overdoing it. When you think you've finished give it a careful look to see if any tones really need to be strengthened, and then stop before you overwork it.

At first you might not be very successful in your efforts but as you continue to practise you will soon develop the necessary skill to make your work look more convincing.

A Still Life with Line and Tone

To set up a simple still-life arrangement, take some ordinary everyday objects that are not too complex in shape. My particular choice has been a tray with a teapot, a jug, a sugar bowl and a cup and saucer and spoon. This has the benefit of being both immediately to hand and familiar. I have put these items on a small tray to limit the area to be drawn. This means that they all overlap each other from my viewpoint, which forces a composition on the picture that I don't have to choose.

◁ Step 1

So now I have my still life in front of me, and I need to assess the whole picture in a simple way that helps me to start the drawing. With very light strokes I indicate the main shapes of the group of objects very loosely, altering and erasing any marks that don't look like the group of shapes I can see. At this stage the main point of the exercise is to get a very simple idea of all the shapes together and their relative sizes and forms.

◁ Step 2

Having arrived at a satisfactory set of forms, I now need to define them more accurately. This means carefully drawing an outline of each object, showing how they overlap each other and how each shape is formed, this time very decisively. I am then left with a complete outline picture of the whole still life. Any obvious mistakes can be carefully redrawn – it is easier to correct the mistake first and then erase the bits that are not correct.

◁ **Step 3**
Now the essence of the picture is complete, I can turn to the tonal values that will help me show the three-dimensional qualities of the forms. At this stage I put only one depth of tone all over, except for areas of white paper to act as highlights. When this is finished the whole picture has taken on a more solid look.

△ **Step 4**
The final stage of the drawing is an exercise in seeing which areas are much darker than all the others and which less dark. I find the best way to deal with this is to do the very darkest areas first and then gradually add any tone required to the less dark places. As you can see, quite large areas have a fairly dark tone, especially the tabletop and the surface of the tray. When I am satisfied that the tones in the drawing match the tones that I can see on the objects, I know that my shading exercise is finished. If any areas are a little too dark I can gently drag an eraser across the tone to lighten it.

This exercise may take you some time to complete, and if you find that it is becoming a chore you should stop and continue some time later – it doesn't matter if it takes longer than one session.

A Still Life with Fruit

Here is another example of a relatively simple still life for you to try. First collect a few pieces of fruit that appeal to you and arrange them on a surface so that some of them are behind others. I've chosen a bunch of grapes, which I've placed further back than the rest of the fruit, and three tomatoes, an apple and a nectarine.

⋀ **Step 1**
Start off by making a very loose sketch to get some idea as to how the arrangement looks. This drawing is not precise and is really to give you a basis on which to start drawing more definitely.

⋀ **Step 2**
In the next stage, draw the shapes of each piece of fruit quite concisely, making sure that each is as accurate as possible. This is the time to do any correcting and erasing, with the hope that it won't then be necessary in any later stages.

∧ **Step 3**
Then carefully put in the areas of tone,
all in a uniformly light tone. With the
larger pieces of fruit, draw the tonal
area with your pencil strokes following
the form of the fruit.

∧ **Step 4**
Now all that is needed is to work over all the tonal areas
until the darkest to lightest values make sense. One way to
see how correct your tonal values are is to half-close your
eyes when you look at the still life, which will help you
to see tone rather than colour. If you have taken the tone
over the highlighted areas by mistake, you can bring those
back by using an eraser to re-establish them.

Drawing Your own Hand

This exercise starts with the simple task of drawing around the outline of your own hand. Just place your hand flat on the paper and then carefully draw all around the shape, making sure that the pencil point does not get too far away from, or too much under, the edge of your hand.

Lift your hand carefully off the paper, keeping it flat and in the same position as before, then draw in all the wrinkles, bumps and hollows that you can see in the simplest way possible, and of course the fingernails too. You will have a fairly good representation of your own hand, matching it for size and shape. Now have a go at drawing it in the same position but without tracing around the edge of it. Does the second drawing look as good as the first one?

The next step is to hold your hand in a different shape, for example showing the palm instead of the back, or with a pointing finger, a clenched fist or any other shape you wish to try out. Take your time doing this, because the effort you put into trying to be accurate to the shapes that you see is the most valuable part of this exercise in drawing.

You are familiar with the look of your own hand, and it is a living object, unlike the previous things that you have been drawing. Don't be worried if your first attempts are a little rough in technique – this is normal if you are a beginner. The skill comes with repeating these sorts of exercises as many times as you can.

Drawing a Head and Face

This exercise is one for which you will need a model. If someone you know will sit for you for an hour you can draw their face, but if this is difficult, simply position yourself in front of a good-sized mirror and draw your own.

∧ Step 1

To start with you need to draw a straight-on, full-face view, so that you can understand the proportions of the human head. Make a mark at the top of the page to indicate where the top of the head is going to be, and another where the point of the chin will go. Don't make the distance between these two points bigger than the size of the head, although it doesn't matter if it is a bit smaller. Now draw a line straight down to join the top mark to the bottom. This indicates the centre of the head vertically. All the shapes you are going to draw should be evenly balanced either side of this line.

Looking carefully at the shape of the head in front of you, whether your own or your model's, have a go at drawing the oval shape of the whole head – and I mean the whole head, not just the face. You'd be surprised how many beginners draw the head as though there is nothing much above the hairline.

∧ Step 2

Draw a horizontal line halfway down the head to show the level of the eyes. Mark in the position and shape of the eyes on this line. The distance between them is the same as the length of the eye from corner to corner.

Then mark in the end of the nose, about halfway between the eyes and the point of the chin. Draw just the nostrils and the bottom edge of the nose. Next draw the line of the mouth, which is slightly nearer the nose than the chin – it is usually positioned at one-fifth of the whole head length from the bottom of the chin. Draw the shape between the lips, then, more lightly, put in the shape of the upper lip below the nose and the fold under the lower one, not the edge of the lip colour.

Mark in the hair, the position of the ears, if they can be seen, and the eyebrows. The tops of the ears and the eyebrows are at about the same level. So now you have the basic head with its features put in.

◁ **Step 3**

The next stage is to erase your guidelines and draw all the features and the hair. Look at the thickness of the eyebrows and note that the shape of the inner corner of the eye is different to that of the outer. You can't see a great deal of the ears from this angle, but try to get the shape as accurately as you can.

The most important areas of the nose are the under part and the shape of the nostrils. There may be a strong shadow showing the bonier part of the nose – but mark it in only lightly, or it will look like a beak.

The mouth is a bit easier, but remember that the strongest marks should be reserved for the line where the lips meet; if you make the edges of the lip colour too strong it will have the effect of flattening the lips.

The outline of the jaw and cheekbones is important to show the characteristics of the face in front of you. If you make the jaw too large or small it will look clumsy or weak respectively, so take your time to get this right.

The hair is also important, especially where it defines the shape of the skull underneath. If it's too big your model will look like an alien, while if it's too small the head will appear to lack enough space for brains.

◁ **Step 4**

Now you can start to mark in the shading on the face and hair, putting it all in at the same strength. There will usually be light coming from one side, and in my example the left side of the face is in some shadow and the right side is in more light. This stage is where the projecting features such as the nose, eyebrows and mouth start to show their form. Shade the hair in the same way, but take the marks in the direction that the hair grows. If the hair is dark, put another layer of tone everywhere except where the light shines strongly on it.

△ Step 5

In the last stage, draw in the very darkest tones and the variety of tones over the whole head. You may have to darken the hair quite a bit, but remember that only the deepest shadows should be black.

Mark in the edges of the eyelids carefully. The edge of the upper lid is much darker than the lower, partly because it is facing downwards and partly because the eyelashes cast a shadow. The pupil of the eye is dark, but usually you can see a bright speck which reflects the light in the room, which gives the eye its sparkle. Note the shadow around the eye near to the nose.

The shading around the nose and the mouth should be done very carefully – if you make it too dark the result will look a bit cartoonish. Try to let the tones melt into each other so that there are no sudden changes. The shading on the sides of the jawline is often darker than on the point of the jaw because the light is reflected back up under the chin. Keep stopping to look at the whole picture to see if you are getting the balance of tone right. Don't be afraid of erasing over and over again to get the right effect – the result may end up a bit messy, but you will have learnt a valuable lesson about form in a drawing.

Showing Materiality

As you get more proficient, you will find that the marks you make when you draw any object give an effect of the material that it is made of. On these pages there are two examples to help you realize this. The first is an exercise often given to art students to test their ability to observe shape and texture, and that is to take a piece of paper, crumple it up, and then put it down and draw it as accurately as you can. The second exercise is to draw a piece of woollen, cotton or silk clothing, showing its texture clearly. When you have finished you will have reached the end of your second week of drawing, and you will have managed to draw many very different objects and discovered how they can be done.

Exercise 1

Start by drawing the crumpled paper in outline so that you have got the whole shape down. Keep the line light and as smooth as you can. When you think your drawing is close enough to the shape in front of you, make any corrections you need to.

Now carefully put in as much of the tonal areas as you can – it is a bit difficult with white paper, because some of the tones are so similar. When all the tones on the paper are done, put in the background tones. As you can see on my example, the wall behind is quite dark, but the paper is resting on a white surface. The dark wall helps to throw the mass of paper forward in space a little, and gives contrast to the rest of the tonal areas.

Exercise 2

◁ **Step 1**
For the piece of clothing, try this knitted cotton sweater draped across the back of a wood and canvas chair. First draw a rough sketch to make sure you have got the mass and bulk of the subject right.

≪ Step 2

Now make a careful outline drawing, allowing the lines to suggest the soft edges of the material as well as the shape of it. Make sure that the hard, smooth lines of the chair contrast with the texture of the sweater's outline.

▷ Step 3

Next make a careful all-over rendering of the main tone, not differentiating between dark and light tones at this stage. Leave white paper where the brightest highlights appear on the sweater.

≪ Step 4

Lastly, build up the tonal values to give an effect of the texture and soft drape of the garment, taking care to make the chair look harder and sharper-edged than the cloth.

WEEK 3 # Choosing Your Subjects

This week you will be expanding your range of subjects and developing your drawings with more attention to detail. The natural world, the human form and man-made objects offer an endless source of material, and most of us don't need to look far to find a subject to draw within these areas.

Starting with plants, you will practise drawing the subtle and fragile shapes of leaves and flowers with much careful observation. That is indeed the most important thing here, because without it you will only be drawing the conventional images of the world that are fixed in your mind. There is nothing wrong with drawing from your imagination in itself, but it will not add much to your drawing skills. These have to be informed by all the new things that you start to see when you are studying forms in some depth.

Next you will draw the human figure and face, at first economically and then in some detail. You will also try sketching some domestic animals, using photographs to capture their poses if necessary. Finally you will try methods of looking at man-made objects in different ways to allow your drawing skills to develop more extensively. As an artist, you will learn to see the world in ways that people lacking strong visual interests don't tend to develop.

All these exercises are similar to those traditionally undertaken by art students, and if you follow them through there's no doubt your drawing will improve. But remember, the more you practise the better you will get; most professional artists don't let a day go by without some form of practice.

Drawing Flowers and Plants

This exercise is designed to set you on the right path to drawing plants and flowers close up. Start with the simplest forms that you feel comfortable with, but don't hesitate to draw something more complex if the subject holds greater interest for you, since that is more important than anything else.

I have started here with a small four-petalled blossom using a soft conté pencil, which leaves a rather chalky line (see page 79 for more about using conté). I've added some tone to the parts in shadow, but kept it all fairly simple.

The next subject I drew was this stalk with leaves. I didn't try to show texture, satisfying myself with the shapes of the leaves and their arrangement on the stalk, with the main veins drawn in as well. Try this, looking only at the outline shape of your plant, but drawing every detail of the edges.

My next drawings are more complex. At first I just drew the strong, well-defined shapes of some unopened lilies, using a conté pencil to get a soft edge without any details of texture.

Next I moved on to an opened blossom, with all its complexity of texture and construction. This required much more attention to the details of tone and textural values, so that the form can be seen clearly. In your own drawing, take this quite slowly because it does require good observation of every detail.

A still life of plants

A plant still life can be either formal or informal – for example, a vase of flowers usually gives a more formal effect than plants in a flowerbed or window box. The one shown here is a large box of various herbs.

⊳ Step 1
Start as usual with a very loose sketch of the main shapes of the plants, getting some idea of the way that they grow and fall.

◁ Step 2
Next comes a line drawing to put in all the leaves and stalks so that the plants are differentiated. At this stage you should make any necessary corrections – although the shapes may be changing all the time if you are working outside in the slightest breeze.

A **Step 3**

Putting in shading will give some depth to the plants. The darkest shadows go in first, then gradually build up the different tonal areas until the result looks fairly realistic. There is no need to draw the smaller leaves exactly – just put them in with an expressive scribble. The contrast between the box and the leaves helps to make the leaves look softer and more fragile.

Drawing a Human Figure

Figure drawing is not so easy as drawing plants, not least because it requires the co-operation of your friends or relatives. Most people don't like to sit still for too long, so you may have to stop drawing sooner than you would wish because your model has got tired of posing. The idea here is to draw a whole figure including the face and clothes, so make sure your model is comfortable before you start and allow them some breaks to move around and stretch cramped muscles.

◁ **Step 2**
The next step is to firm up the main shapes of the figure, paying close attention to the angle of the head, the shape of the arms and hands, and the relaxed turn of the body. By the end of this step the broad outline of the model is established.

△ **Step 1**
First make a simple sketch of the position of the figure on the chair. I was sitting quite close to my subject, so the legs disappear at the lower edge of the picture. Notice how in this initial drawing the main shape of the movement through the body and the arrangement of the arms and head are already shown, albeit briefly.

➤ Step 3

Now it's time to look at the details of each part of the figure, making careful note of the shape of the head and the hair, and the way the features are arranged. Next, the way that the clothes drape around the body needs to be seen clearly, but don't put in every detail of the clothing at this stage – just the main folds that define the form underneath. Put in the hands and the parts of the chair that can be seen; in this case I could see the model's legs so I defined the main shape of these as well.

> **Step 4**

Firm up the shapes of the body and head, so that your model starts to become recognizable. Remember that this is always a work in progress, and you don't have to end up with a highly finished piece of work. Alter or erase anything that you think is not looking like the shapes you can see, and don't worry if the drawing becomes very messy; this just means that you are beginning to observe more sharply, and the effort to correct your drawing is never wasted.

Notice that on my finished drawing the marks are very exploratory – the edge of the body is drawn with a variety of lines, not sharply defined. This allows for the fact that you can see around the edges of a three-dimensional form and so there is never really one sharp line. I have not put in much texture or shading, just enough to show the form in a simple fashion. It is still a drawing in progress, and if I could get my model to sit again in exactly the same position with the same clothes on, I could continue drawing for another period of time.

Drawing Facial Features

Having tried a facial portrait in Week 2 (see page 28) and looked at the human figure (see page 37), your next exercise is to look at the features of the face in some detail. The face is normally our first point of recognition when we see people, so it is important to familiarize yourself with the features and draw them with confidence.

Eyes

The most significant part of the face that we recognize is the eyes, so we will start there. You can begin by drawing only one eye, but it's probably a good idea to draw both together so that the relationship of the two eyes to each other is observed.

▷ My first drawing is of the eyes of a young woman who is looking to one side. Notice how the inner shape of the corner of the eye is different to that of the outer corner and how the eyes are set slightly around the curve of the head. Draw the eyebrows as well so that the space between the eyes can be judged more easily. This girl's eyes are looking up towards the light, so they are not open wide – the iris (the coloured part of the eye) is covered slightly by the upper lid and is touching, if not slightly under, the lower lid, something that is often not observed by beginners.

Now try drawing one eye, taking note of every detail of its shape and construction. I have drawn a diagram of the eye as well to emphasize its form. Note that the inner corner has the tear duct hollow, while the outer corner is simpler. The thickness of the eyelid can be seen on both the upper and lower lid, and they curve over the eyeball; the iris and the pupil curve too. The pupil will of course enlarge or diminish according to how much light is shining on the eye.

Mouths

Mouths are the next most recognizable part of the human face, except in the case of someone with a really dramatic nose. Draw mouths both shut and slightly open to understand the formation of the lips; the lower lip is often thicker than the upper one, but this is not invariably the case.

Noses

There is a lot of variation in noses, and they often form a very characterful part of the face. They are not at all hard to draw in profile, but quite tricky full-face.

It's easiest to describe the shape from the front when there is a strong light coming from one side to cast a shadow.

Most noses come in three or four types: the snub or retroussé nose, the straight nose, the strong, curved nose or the broken nose. The straight nose is probably the most difficult to draw because of the lack of bumps or indentations. Most beginners tend to make their subject's nose too long or too short, so observe it carefully in relation to the rest of the face.

Ears

Ears are often neglected in a portrait because long hair is partially hiding them or because we rarely look at them. Indeed, most of us would be hard pushed to recognize the ears of even our nearest and dearest.

Here are a few examples of different ears and you should have a go at several, because they do have various shapes. The construction is basically the same, but the details differ. Draw some ears from the side and then from the front as well to get some idea of how they look.

Drawing Animals

Drawing animals is not unlike drawing human figures in that you will find yourself dealing with the same issues of getting the proportions and features correct. The major difference, of course, is that you won't be able to persuade any animal to stay patiently in a pose you choose. Indeed, many won't remain still long enough for you to manage any more than a quick sketch. This means that you have to start drawing quickly and go for only the most obvious shapes first, even in the case of a sleeping animal, as most tend to move quickly once awake.

This is an area of drawing where photography is particularly useful, especially for supplementing swift sketches done at the same time. Taking photographs of the animals in similar poses to the ones you have tried to capture will give you the information to do a more finished drawing. However, it's probable that to familiarize yourself with drawing animals you will have to start by resorting to books or magazines that give you either detailed photographs of animals or drawings by artists who have specialized in the subject.

Cats

Domestic cats are very useful models as they are very somnolent – most sleep for about 16 hours a day. Consequently, you should have plenty of time for fairly detailed studies and because of their furry coat and relaxed, graceful forms they present easy, fluid shapes to draw. Draw the main shape of the pose in a very simple way, as you can see in these examples, and add the texture of the fur with multiple strokes of the pencil. When you feel confident enough, try drawing some more active animals.

Dogs

Dogs spend less time asleep than cats but, while awake, tend to be much more co-operative. They vary much more in appearance, so you will need to check the proportions with each new breed to make it recognizable. As before, draw the main shape simply at first and add detail with strokes of your pencil.

Drawing Larger Objects

You have practised drawing small objects such as cups and cutlery to give you the idea of showing man-made forms – now it's time to tackle larger objects that are often functional and complex. Of course the largest objects made by man are architectural or major works of engineering, but for the time being we will look at items such as vehicles and furniture.

Exercise 1

Start with a car – either your own or one that is close enough for you to draw it easily. First do a fairly simple drawing of the car from the side, the most recognizable view of a car shape.

Lightly block out a roughly rectangular shape that encompasses the length and height of the vehicle and mark in the position of the wheels, the line of the windows, and the slope of the

bonnet and back. Then carefully draw in all the main parts of the machine, including the door handles, wing mirrors, wheel hubs, lights and even an indication of the headrests of the seats inside. The main focus here is not artistic beauty but literal precision in the placing of all the parts of the vehicle and their proportions, more like a technical drawing.

Now take up a new position where you can see the car from three-quarters front and side view. This is a lot harder to draw and you may have to refer back to your profile view to check that you are placing things correctly. The hardest part will be getting the proportion right, since the parts nearer to you will appear much larger than the parts further back.

Exercise 2

Having drawn the car to the best of your ability, try a bicycle, which is still difficult but has less bulk to include. Basically, a bicycle is already like a line drawing because everything is in linear mode, unlike the larger surfaces of a car. Don't get caught up in the idea of getting each detail perfect – just go for the main construction of the frame and wheels.

You can emphasize some edges to give extra weight to the appearance of the wheels or frame. The handlebars and the back wheel are more strongly drawn here.

WEEK 4 The Outside
World

This week the emphasis is on going out of your house to explore the surrounding landscape as a subject. You will begin to place objects in the larger scheme of things and start to understand how a whole scene can be handled. While drawing landscapes is not much different in essence from drawing anything else, the sheer scale of the view is sometimes a bit daunting, so you will need to find ways of tackling that.

You may find that the exercises take longer to work through because of the nature of the subject matter, so try to set aside time to enjoy them and not feel rushed. For your first landscape view, I recommend a site close to home that is familiar to you. This has the advantage that if you do not finish your drawing in one session you can easily return to the same spot.

One thing that you may find difficult is that when you are drawing in public places, someone will almost certainly want to see what you are doing. In the main I find that people are quite polite about this, but if you find the attention unnerving, remember that the opinions that matter are those of your teacher and fellow students, and your own. In fact you have become your own teacher with the help of this book, so steel yourself to disregard any uncomplimentary remarks – what matters is that you keep drawing.

We will be returning to landscapes in Week 10 (pages 131–143), so there will be more opportunity to consolidate your skills.

Water and Plants

Finding a path into drawing a whole landscape is made so much easier by looking closely at its fundamental parts and realizing that a pebble, a rock and a mountain are effectively the same forms on a different scale, just as a leaf and stalk on a houseplant is a miniature version of a tree and a puddle is a tiny lake.

Make an easy start by dropping a little water on to a flat, plain surface that won't absorb the moisture – I used my kitchen worktop. What you will then have is a very small pool of water that reflects the light. Draw carefully around the outline shape, then put in any tone that you can see, shading it with your pencil. It will probably be quite simple, as you can see that my puddle was. There were a few tiny outer splashes of water as well, which I put in – adding any extra details like this will help you to get the feel of water and its properties.

Now return to drawing plants again to get a clearer idea of how they work visually. I have drawn just two bunches of leaves that were growing in my road – I could have drawn much more from what was there, but this was quite good enough to get my hand in for drawing vegetation. You will have to decide how much you need to draw in order to feel confident.

48

Next I turned my attention to a large pot of hydrangeas to study larger, well-defined leaves. This time I concentrated on the basic shapes as they lay across each other and the varied shadows they created.

This drawing of a pine tree uses simple pencil strokes to represent the texture of the foliage. Note how I have put in some marks that resemble branches, to help show the structure of the tree. In some parts I have made the marks darker to denote deeper shadow.

This drawing shows the surface of a small pond. To achieve the glassy quality of the still water, lay your marks down smoothly in horizontal strokes, leaving areas of light, and put in darker tones around the edges.

Trees

Continuing from the previous exercise, we stay with the natural world but tackle a much larger subject in the form of trees. This will require you to go outdoors to draw unless you have good views of whole trees from your window. Don't try to bite off more than you can chew at this stage – just choose trees that you can see easily in one glance.

I started with a fairly loose rendition of a tree, drawing the trunk and branches first and then marking in the main bulk of the vegetation with broad, scribbly strokes, using a very soft pencil (6B). Notice that there is no detail at all in this drawing – I was content to show just the main shape.

My next drawing is a bit sharper in tone, mainly because it is a pine tree seen against the sunlight, which almost reduces the tree to a silhouette. The shape of this tree was very distinct and quite simple, so it did not tax my powers of concentration too much. What did seem to be important was the upcurving shape of the branches and the rather sharp edge of the shapes.

Try drawing the trees shown here first, then translate what you have learnt to real life and also have a go at close-ups of branches from different trees, describing how they look growing out of the trunk and standing out against the sky.

A Scene Close to Home

Now I want you to tackle a landscape drawing that can be done close to where you live. Pick a nice day when you won't have to be struggling with the wind or trying to protect your drawing from the rain – the idea is to make things as easy as possible for yourself on your first attempt to draw a real landscape.

Getting prepared

Before you go out, think about what you will need and what you plan to draw. Take a sketchpad that you will find easy to use – I recommend nothing larger than A3 or smaller than A4. Have at least half a dozen well-sharpened pencils, an eraser and a viewfinder. The latter is easily made by cutting a hole similar to the proportion of your sketchbook in a small piece of card. It is invaluable for landscape drawing, as you can look through it and move it around until you find the composition you want, cutting out all surrounding detail that might distract you. If you forget to take a viewfinder you can form your hands as shown to give a similar effect, but the cut-out version is easier to use.

◁ Step 1

Next you must decide what you want to draw. I was able to see a perfectly good expanse of landscape from my bedroom window, but you might have to be a little more adventurous! I was lucky enough to have a large tree dividing the scene about a third of the way along the picture, and the sun was much stronger on the right side of the scene than on the left side. This allowed a darker tonal value to almost one third of the picture and sharpened up the details of the other part.

⋏ Step 2

I drew the tree shape first and then the line of the rooftops afterwards. I worked over the left side of the work first and then concentrated on the details of the right side. This enabled me to decide just how dark the darker tones were going to be to create the right balance of interest.

Take your time on your own drawing, because the care and attention you give it are all part of working your way towards being an accomplished artist.

△ **Step 3**

When you come to describe the solidity of the buildings and the tree trunk, you can use your shading techniques to explain the textural qualities as well. For example, the roof tiles will look more convincing if your tone is put on with horizontal strokes, with a slight undulation to them to suggest the ridges of the tiles. The vegetation, as in the hedge in front, can be shaded with scribbly marks to suggest the myriad leaf-tips. Try to make the marks on the tree trunk a bit broken to suggest the roughness of the bark. Each area of shading can reinforce the quality of the elements in the picture in this way.

An Expanse of Water

This exercise will require your total concentration and all of the drawing skills you have acquired so far. My drawing is of a small English river, in Sussex. I haven't included much landscape around it, so the only real problem is drawing the water – but this is quite a problem, partly because it is moving, as opposed to the flat surface of a lake on a windless day. I picked a very calm day so that the movement was reduced to a minimum, but even so your task is not an easy one.

Notice how the reflections of the bank and the building upon it are making a darker tone across the surface of the water, but everything is broken up by the ripples, which reflect the light and shade in various ways. The darker tones of the larger ripples help to define the surface so don't hesitate to put in as many of these as you can see, but show the difference between the brighter part of the water and the darker part.

Don't be afraid to put in the very darkest tones, because one of the properties of water is to reflect the lights and darks in quite strong contrasts. It will require some judgement on your part to get the right balance of the tonal values – that is, the difference between the tones from the darkest to the lightest. Take a bit of time calculating these differences – it is never wasted.

An Urban Scene

An urban scene can be just as picturesque and interesting as the countryside. For a start, draw urban details that are easy for you to see, just as you drew individual patches of water and vegetation before embarking on your first landscape.

Preliminary drawings

I have made a selection of the upper parts of a doorway with ironwork protecting and decorating it, a set of chimney pots, and finally a roof eave with a window and drainpipes. However, you don't have to limit yourself to buildings – anything that takes your attention as you are wandering about is fair game, even if it is just a dustbin by a gate or a garden fence. You can find inspiration and interest everywhere if you look with an inquisitive eye.

Looking up at the details of a roof is not so easy, and it is difficult to get the perspective right. But one or two goes at it will soon make you more confident.

Once you've spent some time accustoming yourself to urban details, you will probably decide you want to have a go at a typical urban scene. I went to central London on an autumn day and took up a viewpoint at the end of a short street in Soho with shops and restaurants on either side.

◁ Step 1
First I sketched in the main shapes of the street, indicating parked cars and one or two figures. The same figures wouldn't be there when I finished, but there would be others that I could impose on the same spot.

▷ Step 2
During the time I was drawing the daylight started to fade and the streetlights came on, so I worked up the tonal differences between the illuminated shop windows and streetlights and the dark masses of buildings and trees in the distance. Darkening the sky made the lights appear that much brighter in contrast. I included the tones of the reflections on the damp pavements.

∧ **Step 3**

Having built up the main areas, I could now work a little more subtly to bring out the atmosphere in the night street. Notice how the details of the windows in the buildings become mere dark marks along the receding facades of the houses. Finally, I put in the very darkest tones to sharpen up the whole scene.

Combining Water and Architecture

In this exercise, you will set yourself a challenge by using your experience of drawing water and architecture in one scene. This may entail some planning on your part in order to find the right spot; I am lucky to live close to the River Thames, so there is plenty of choice for me in this respect. I picked a view of Hammersmith Bridge, which is in an urban area, so there is plenty to draw.

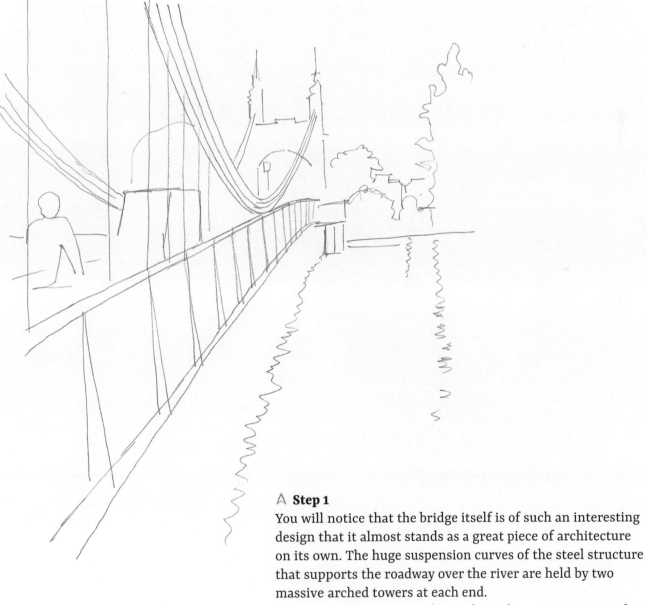

A Step 1

You will notice that the bridge itself is of such an interesting design that it almost stands as a great piece of architecture on its own. The huge suspension curves of the steel structure that supports the roadway over the river are held by two massive arched towers at each end.

I started by drawing in linear form the main structure that I could see and the line of the water with the edges of the main dark reflections.

59

∧ Step 2

Then it was simply a matter of carefully putting in all the texture and construction of the bridge first and adding the background and water effects after.

The very strong shadows on the main parts of the bridge and the deep shadow below it create a striking and interesting image. The water was as difficult as ever, but because I had opted to draw only a narrow part of the further shore it wasn't quite the problem it might have been.

WEEK 5

The Human Figure

This week we come to one of the most interesting, most subtle and most taxing of our drawing challenges. The human figure is the one subject that we all think we know about, because we are humans ourselves. However, because of our close connection with the subject, it's easier not only to follow our preconceptions rather than relying on observation, but also then to realize we have got things wrong. It's consequently rather more difficult to satisfy our own demands of our skill, but that's not a bad thing because it pushes us to strive harder to achieve what we want.

There are many approaches to this field of drawing, and I have started with a method that is easy to understand and achieve. You will see how to simplify your drawing by blocking in the main shapes of the figure before starting to add detail. We will also look at how perspective can subtly alter your view of the figure and how you can go about drawing your own full figure portrait.

Finally, of course, it will be your own observation that will increase your drawing skill in this subject, as in others. You will need the co-operation of your friends and family in this series of exercises, but you will find that most people are happy to oblige.

Proportions of the Figure

Obviously people vary in their exact proportions, but using the head as the basic unit, the average man or woman, fully grown, is about 7½ to 7¾ heads tall. However, most drawings and paintings of human beings can be drawn simply as if 8 units made up the height. This would probably be true of a tall person and so is not too out of proportion – in fact it was the measure generally used for beautiful or heroic figures in art history, so you will not find your models complaining!

The male and female hardly differ at all in their height proportions, but there is a difference in width; the male figure is wider at the shoulders, the female wider at the hips.

Male figure: front view

O UNITS

1

2

3

4

5

6

7

8

Female figure: side view

Child (9–10 years old): front view

A child's head is much bigger in proportion to the body. At one year old it is about 3 to 1 and as they grow the proportions gradually approach those of an adult. At about 9 or 10 years old, a child will be about 6 units or heads to the full height.

Drawing Simple Figures

For looking at the human figure more extensively, you will find that a good supply of photographs of people in action can be very useful. While the best drawings are done only from life, using photographs, especially if you have taken them yourself, is not a bad substitute.

First of all, limit yourself strictly to the simplest way of showing the figure, starting with a blocked shape of the main forms and adding a little detail. In these figures the movement is not great, as befits a first attempt, and two of them were taken from photographs. Try to do a few drawings like this, spending just 3–4 minutes on each one and making your lines fluid and instantaneous, even if at first the results look terrible. All artists start like that, and only time and repeated practice effect a change.

Expressive Figures and Foreshortened Figures

Here we are still looking at the human form, but in poses that are more expressive. The figures on this page are not even shown in full, because my interest is in the gesticulating hands. Once again these might be easier for you to draw from photographs that have frozen the moment.

Block these in to start with as you did before, but pay particular attention to the position of the hands. One woman looks as if she is ticking off points on her fingers, one man is gesturing to draw attention to something and the other woman is raising one hand to comb her hair.

The next drawings look at figures which are lying and sitting in such a way that some of their limbs are foreshortened, making your task more difficult. Remember to observe closely and draw what you can really see, not your assumptions about how a figure should look.

The first woman sits with her legs folded under her, supporting herself with her hands. Her feet and knees project forwards from her trunk and are shown proportionately larger.

The woman lying down holding her knees is seen from quite an unusual angle. Closely study the proportions of her arms and legs to get the foreshortening right.

The last figure, sitting on a stool, is relatively straightforward where the legs are concerned, but the folded arms pose a foreshortening problem. The elbow closest to us is larger than you might expect, and the forearm recedes steeply into the crook of the other arm.

The Limbs and Extremities

On these pages, we'll look at the limbs, hands and feet in more detail. You won't necessarily draw all these particular poses, but try as many as you can before moving on to the next stage. Again it is of more benefit if you can draw from life, and in most cases you could use yourself as the model with the use of a large mirror.

Arms and hands

First, draw some arms from different angles. Those that I've drawn are both feminine and masculine, but if you are drawing your own arms, that doesn't matter at the moment; male and female arms look different, but the basic anatomy is the same.

In my drawings I've shown both the use of tone and a more linear approach to define the form. No matter how many arms you draw, there will always be more to discover about their formation in different positions. If you become really interested in the construction of the human body, you'll find that a good book on anatomy for artists is invaluable.

The hand is a study in itself. Repeating the exercise of tracing round your own hand (see page 26) will help to remind you of its basic shape.

Legs and feet

To draw the legs and feet, again you can use your own seen in a mirror or ask people to pose for you. You will need to show the difference between female and male legs, which is evident in the softer, rounder forms of the former and the harder lines of the latter. However, the difference may not be so obvious on the legs of a female athlete compared to the legs of a sedentary male. The hardest part is to get the proportion between the upper and lower leg correct, and the drawings of the knee and ankle joints.

Draw the legs from various angles: front, back, side and crossed over each other. This helps you to see how the various groups of muscles behave from different angles. When the legs are under more tension the muscles will appear more prominent. The knee joint and the area where the foot joins the leg are quite tricky to get right and it is worth making several studies of them.

Feet are not too difficult in themselves, being less flexible than hands, but the difficult angles are drawing them from directly in front or from the rear.

Drawing the Whole Figure

Drawing the complete human body is really the subject of a life class. Generally speaking, the best you will be able to coax from friends and family is a pose in a bathing costume, since other than the young and beautiful most people are too self-conscious to subject themselves to such scrutiny. This is sufficient for a general view of the body, but if you need to study it more closely in order to understand the bones and muscles showing on the surface a tutored course in life drawing is the obvious answer. While these vary, most of the tuition in such classes is good, because they are usually run by expert art teachers. The complete body is definitely the hardest thing that you will ever draw, and you will find that after a time spent studying it your drawing of other things will also improve. So start with the details of bodies, and then graduate to the complete figure.

A standing position with no foreshortening is easiest, but you will also need to draw models sitting, reclining and also in various more complex poses where the limbs and torso are turned, folded and twisted to show how the different parts of the structure function together. Try to draw from models of different shapes, sizes and ages where possible. One very good way to gain an understanding of the structure of the body is to have the model sitting on a revolving chair and gradually turn it around so that you are drawing the figure in the same pose from a variety of positions.

Any study of the human figure will do wonders for your powers of concentration and your ability to draw any other subject.

The Head: Practice

The following exercise will be to draw a complete portrait of someone, and you need practice on the head to make a success of this. Below are drawings of the head both in profile and full face, with measurements to give you the basic proportions. Although my example is a female head, the same proportions apply to the male. Of course these are generalities, but the differences in proportion in individual heads are so small that it is a good basic set of measurements.

The full-face version shows that the head is longer vertically than horizontally. You can also see that the eyes are halfway down from the top of the head. The length of the nose is about half this again, but the mouth is closer to the nose than to the chin. The widest part of the head is just above the ears and the eyes are the same distance apart as the length of the eye from corner to corner.

On the profile drawing, the hairline is positioned at about half the area of the head on a diagonal basis. The shape of the head is about the same distance across horizontally as it is in length, ignoring the projection of the nose. The ear is just behind the halfway vertical. Note that both in profile and full face the distance of the mouth to the chin and the hairline to the top of the head is about one fifth of the whole length of the head.

71

Now for a few examples of heads in different positions which you will need to study, because you won't necessarily find your subjects' heads in exactly the full-face or profile version. Some of these are seen from slightly below and some from slightly above. The former show the projection of the jaw and the nose seems to be shorter and almost blocking out some of the eye; the latter show more of the top of the head and the mouth tends to disappear under the projection of the nose.

The drawings at the top are all done as blocked-out shapes, emphasizing the three-dimensional quality of the head and getting across the idea of the whole shape, not just the face. If you are a beginner this form of drawing is important for you because it begins to make you see the complete volume of the head, which few non-artists think about.

The drawings underneath show the same head positions, with the hair and features put in more naturally. Notice how the shadows on the faces give an extra dimension, not only to the form but also to the expressions.

Try to draw as many different versions of heads as you can, because it will improve your ability to draw portraits in more depth.

A Full-Figure Portrait

This exercise will seem like a reward for all your hard work so far on the human figure – drawing a complete portrait of someone who will be prepared to pose for you for a while. I took as my model my six-year-old grandson, who is not easy to keep in one position, but I put him in front of the television to watch a film that I knew would interest him so he sat for a little longer than usual. That in itself is a lesson – make your models comfortable and happy and you will get more time to draw them!

∧ Step 1
At first you will need to draw the main shape of the figure. Keep it very simple to start with and use your eraser, correcting as much as you can at this stage – it saves time later on.

∧ Step 2
The next stage is to put in all the shadows that seem relevant, again keeping everything simple – but it is at this stage that the face needs to become recognizable.

△ Step 3

Once you are sure everything is the right shape and in the correct proportion, begin to work into the picture to make it come to life. Take great care over the head, because this is where the picture becomes a portrait of a particular individual rather than of just anyone. This is not so difficult as it sounds because we all have this marvellous ability to recognize human faces, so you will automatically draw the features correctly if you really pay attention. Build up the tones in such a way as to stress the softness or hardness of the form. Good luck in your efforts – even if you are not successful this time, the practice will enable you to do a lot better on the next occasion, and we'll be looking at portrait drawing in more detail in Week 9 (pages 117–130).

Materials and Techniques

Now that you have explored many of the main subject areas of drawing, this week you will start to try out the different mediums available to you, all of them traditional. In each exercise I have demonstrated how you might handle the medium, but I have by no means exhausted the possibilities. While every medium has a different influence on the method of drawing, when you have become more confident with them through constant practice you will find it interesting to overlap your techniques and tools in the spirit of ongoing experimentation.

What will eventually dictate your choice of medium for any particular picture is how well it suits the subject matter and the way you like to draw. Even when you have found one you especially enjoy working with, don't stop there – keep on trying out different methods and mediums to expand your repertoire and become fluent in any you favour. This is all part of the artist's technical trade, and although that may sound a bit mundane, in fact it is where the fun intermingles with all the hard work.

Pencils

In the first two exercises you will be exploring different types of pencil and the tools that accompany their use. I recommend that you work with the following: pencils in grades B, 2B, 4B and 6B; a clutch, or propelling, pencil that takes a 0.5mm lead, which will give you a line of constant width; and a graphic stick of either 2B or 4B grade to use for large strokes and a soft build-up of tone. You will also require an eraser both to remove unwanted marks and to create highlights in a tonal area. A kneadable putty eraser is good, but a soft normal eraser is useful as well; I use both types. Avoid very hard erasers, which tend to tear the surface of the paper.

A stump or paper stub, which is a tool designed for smudging pencil work, will help you to obtain a smooth tone of grey. The size isn't too important, but a thin one and a thicker one would be useful.

Pencil: using line

For this large basket of fruit, the aim is to use your pencil line to show the solidity of the shapes, rather than adding tone. First of all, map out the main shapes and correct any obvious mistakes with your eraser. When you are satisfied with your outline go over it carefully, building the denser tones around the shapes of the fruit and basket so that you begin to show a more intense version of their volume. Keep the drawing to the least possible needed to show the solidity of the shapes. This is rather like the way Cézanne built up the substance of his drawings.

Pencil: adding tone

Now we go for the tonal values of a drawing – that is, in this next drawing you will start by delineating the outline first and then going on to build up the drawing tonally in areas of shading and texture. Here the point is not to emphasize the edge, or linear look, of the drawing, but the light and shade at the expense of the line. When you have finished, the drawing should look as though there are no obvious lines, just areas of tone in different depths.

≪ Step 1

I have chosen an armchair under the light of a window because the shapes are large and relatively simple. This enables me to avoid becoming too caught up in the details of the linear form, as all the shapes are easy to draw. Keep your own outlines as simple as possible and avoid any fiddly detail.

≻ Step 2

Now choose a tone that corresponds to the lightest tone in the picture other than the highlights, and put this uniformly over every area except where there are highlights, leaving those as untouched white paper.

◁ Step 3

Having done this, you no longer have the outline as the dominant characteristic but large areas of light tone to deal with. Now, very carefully, build up the darker tones until you have a well-defined mass of tonal values that show you the main shapes of the form.

▷ Step 4

The rest of your task is to gradually build up each area of tone until the greater subtleties of the form begin to show. Continue until you are satisfied that your drawing looks like the actual forms in front of you. This can take a long time – maybe two or three hours – but it's great fun and very valuable to your practice.

Pastels

Pastel is a time-honoured medium in all its various guises, which include soft chalks and charcoal. The very softest pastels, which are usually rounded in section, are favoured by many artists, but they are expensive and are used up quite quickly. There are harder versions which are very good; these usually come in a rectangular section.

The type of charcoal most often used is known as willow charcoal, which has a very soft texture. This can be employed for any kind of drawing but tends to work best on a large scale. You can easily smudge it with your fingers or a paper stump to create a smokey tone. Ideally, you should equip yourself with sticks of varying widths and try them out first on a spare piece of paper as charcoal is quite crumbly if used too heavily – indeed, one of its great advantages is that it makes you handle your medium lightly. It can also cover the paper quickly and, if applied lightly, is easy to erase.

Conté is a form of compressed graphite or charcoal which is simple to use and doesn't crumble too easily but is hard to erase. It also comes in a pencil form, sometimes called charcoal pencils. These are not quite so versatile as the stick form but are cleaner to handle.

Charcoal and conté smudge easily, so you will need some good fixative to spray over your drawing after it is finished. This is available from art supplies shops.

Pastel: adding tone

> **Step 1**

I made this drawing using a conté pastel. To make your task easier, draw from a photograph rather than from a real person. Make sure the photograph is a good one with plenty of tone in it. One of the problems with using photographs for reference is that they never give you as much information as your eye gains from real life, but for the purposes of this exercise that's an advantage because it allows you to analyse the tones more easily.

Remembering that in this medium you cannot erase your lines much, draw in the main outline shapes of the face and head.

< Step 2
Then, as you did with the chair on pages 77–78, put a single tone across the whole picture where there is tone on the photograph, keeping it as light as possible. You may want to place a piece of paper underneath your drawing hand to prevent smudging.

< Step 3
Lastly, build up the stronger tones so that the picture starts to look like the photo you have been copying. Leave white areas for the brightest highlights on the hair, in the eyes and on the face. These will bring life to your drawing.

Pen and Ink

In this medium the line is paramount, and the tonal areas are built up with multiple lines. Because of this it is a slow medium for large drawings, but ideal for very small ones on account of the fineness of its marks.

There are many varieties of pen and ink to use, the traditional one being Indian ink applied with a dip pen. This ink is available in both permanent and watersoluble forms. I find acrylic versions of it less good because they can gum up the pen nib. Indian ink is very black and definite, but the watersoluble type can be thinned to almost any degree of tone.

You will need to use a dip pen with a fine pointed nib designed for drawing, as opposed to calligraphy, for example. These can be bought in art supplies shops and other specialist outlets. The nibs come in several sizes and qualities of fineness, so you might have to experiment before you find the size you prefer. I always use the finest point I can obtain, but that's my preference.

There are also numerous graphic pens with their own ink supply and nibs in various grades of fineness. The one I use the most is the finest one, which is 0.1, but I sometimes also use grades 0.3, 0.5 and 0.8. Again you should try out different sizes to see which you prefer. The only drawback to these pens is that you have to throw them away when they run out of ink. A bottle of ink and a dip pen will last much longer and can be finer even than a 0.1.

For large areas of black you will need a large marker pen. These come in varying sizes and use the same sort of ink as the finer graphic pens.

Now for some drawing. First try this sphere or ball, apparently sitting on a surface with a dark background. This was not drawn from life but is a construct based on observation as to how light shows the shape of a spherical object. Notice how the texture of the tones is built up with numerous fine lines crossing over each other. This technique, called cross-hatching, can be controlled to show both light and dark tones – if you persevered you could ultimately achieve a solidly black surface.

The trick of this type of illusion is to space your lines carefully so that the difference between the darkest and lightest tones is subtly graduated. Notice how putting the sphere against a dark background helps to throw it forward in the apparent space, and how the crescent of tone defining the sphere is darkest not at the very edge but slightly in from it. This imitates the reflection from the surface of the plane the sphere is resting on.

A still life in pen and ink

In this exercise you are going to take on the challenge of drawing a complete composition in pen and ink. Don't attempt a large-scale drawing at first – when you are more practised in the medium you can expand the size of your drawings, but it will take time.

I took a fairly simple still-life composition which does however have quite dark tones in it. This means that I had to work quite fast to get all the areas of tone built up to my satisfaction. If you want to avoid a lot of mark-making, choose a more brightly lit subject.

One of the tricky things about ink is its finality, which means that before you start on the ink drawing you may want to draw the outline in pencil to ensure that you have got the shapes right. This is how most commercial drawing in ink is done. You can then rub out the pencil before you proceed with the rest of the drawing.

> **Step 1**
Having produced a pencil outline of your composition, go over it very lightly in ink as shown here.

◁ **Step 2**
Then build a simple light tone over all the parts that are not highlighted, using vertical lines. As you can see the outline almost disappears when you do this, so don't make your lines too heavy or you will find it hard to see your composition amid the tone.

∧ Step 3

Now comes the build-up. Put in the slightly darker tone with multiple diagonal lines and then the next darkest with horizontal lines and so on, with lines going in the opposite diagonal to build even denser shadows. When you have done lines vertically, horizontally and in both diagonals, you will have to use strokes going in as many directions as you can to build up the very darkest shadows. Use curved lines as well and scribbly marks to fill up any areas that look too light in tone. This will all take quite some time, so you have to be prepared to put aside time for this medium.

Brush and Wash

The technique of brush and wash is rather like traditional watercolour painting but without the colour, being only black and tones of grey.

For working in this medium you will need: black watercolour pigment or black watersoluble ink; a china or plastic watercolour palette in which to dilute your pigment or ink; a jar for water, preferably glass so that you can easily see when you need to change the water (for a long session of work two jars are useful); and at least two brushes, sizes 2 and 10, to start with (later you may wish to add a size 6 and a really fat brush, especially as you get more expert). These should ideally be sable round brushes, which hold the most liquid and come to the best point and are correspondingly expensive, but if you don't want to spend large sums until you are sure you enjoy using the medium you can buy squirrel hair, or even nylon, which are adequate but lose their point fairly soon.

Remember that for a water-based medium like this you will need to use heavy-weight cartridge paper, as thin paper will cockle when you add water.

The first exercise is to draw in line with the brush. I drew this old horse using a fat brush, but you might find it easier to start with a thinner brush. As you can see, the quality of the line is quite different to all the other mediums that you've used so far. After a few trials you will be able to control the thickness of the line, but not entirely – half the fun is that this medium gives some very attractive variations on what you expect.

Now take an object and have a go at putting in the tones, using the larger brush to apply your liquid quickly enough before it dries. The blending of tones is quite easy when it is still wet, but for the darker, more defined marks I waited until my paint had dried. You have to be both fast and patient with this medium.

A still life in brush and wash

Having had some practice, you should feel confident enough with your handling of the brush to try something a bit more ambitious. I have chosen to use the same still life that figures in the pen and ink exercise on pages 82–83. This way you can see how vastly the two techniques differ, while both arriving at an interesting result.

> **Step 1**
First you will have to draw out the shapes you are going to use with the thinnest brush, but if you are still doubtful of your ability to do this, just draw in pencil first and then go over it with the brush. Erase any pencil work left showing before you continue.

△ **Step 2**
Then mix a very light wash and apply it over every area of shadow in the picture. Leave only the very brightest areas of paper white and make sure you do not cover them over in subsequent layers.

∧ Step 3

Now gradually build up the tones until you get to the deepest black where it is needed. If you want the tones to blend softly, then add paint before your first layer is dry. If you want a sharp line, then wait until your paint is dry before adding it. Be careful here, as it is easy to darken tone too quickly and then find you have overdone it. And there you have your complete composition, which you can compare with your pencil, pastel and pen and ink drawings.

Mixed Media

The last technique we are going to explore this week is working with mixed media, combining some of the techniques used so far and also introducing collage with paper.

This view along the River Thames near Twickenham was drawn in summer, which in my view is the best time for drawing landscape in England. Try to find a similar scene to draw from life using a range of materials or, if that is not possible, copy my example.

First, using a pencil, I lightly sketched the outline of the whole scene and then proceeded to work from the top downwards.

All the area above the foreground wall was done in wash and brush, achieving as much subtlety in the scene as I could. When this was dry, I added a few pen and ink marks to

the boats gathered by the side of the river. I carefully built up a texture in pencil over the whole of the vegetation growing over the wall, and put in some similar marks to indicate the brickwork on the wall and grass on the lawn.

Having done this I then covered the area of the wall and its shadow on the grass using a watercolour wash, making the shadow slightly darker than the wall.

Finally I scrawled in the wall vegetation with a charcoal pencil in order to give it a coarser texture than that of all the other vegetation, smudging it slightly with my thumb.

This larger composition is of architecture and trees in Eccleston Square in London. Choose a similar scene of buildings and trees near to your own home – one that you can stand back from to view it at a reasonable distance.

Here I started by placing on the left-hand side of the picture a piece of paper that was cut out on the inner side and torn on the outer. This would form the building in the foreground of my picture. I stuck this down with paper glue so that I could work on top of it.

Using a pencil, I drew in all the main lines of the windows, trees and railings. Then I went over the buildings in pen and ink, some parts quite sketchily and other parts more well-defined.

With a conté pencil I marked in the large trees and vegetation, and some of the tones on the collage. Then, with a brush, I washed in the larger shadows on all the buildings and over the conté scribble of the trees and other vegetation. I used two tones of watercolour wash to achieve an effect of depth.

Using Perspective

As yet we have only considered perspective very briefly, so this week we will deal with it in more detail as it's an essential part of drawing visually believable pictures. The principles are not too difficult to understand and master, but some practice will be required before it becomes second nature and you are able to use perspective almost without thinking about it.

The first stages of learning about perspective are very theoretical and until you begin to apply it in practice you'll probably find it rather confusing; it's also not totally convincing without the application of direct observation as well. That is why those computer-generated, apparently three-dimensional pictures always look slightly unreal. They work at a glance but if you have time to study them they don't have quite the subtlety that the observed world does.

With a bit of practice at drawing perspective you'll soon begin to see how it works in real life and you'll be able to make all the subtle adjustments that help to make your drawings more convincing. It may seem a rather dry topic, but do make sure you can handle this systematic rendering of the visual world before you get into the habit of drawing things that just don't look quite right to the viewer.

One-Point Perspective

The first exercise deals with what is called one-point perspective. This means that there is only one point on the horizon line that all the main lines of the composition lead to. All other lines will be either horizontal or vertical.

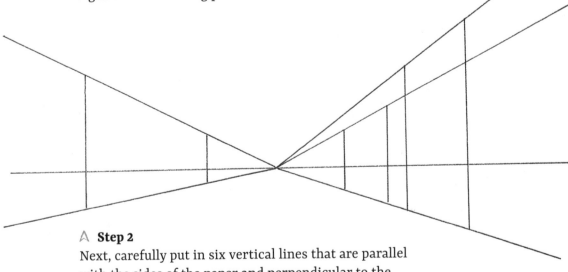

∧ **Step 1**
Start by drawing the horizon line across the page; in real life, the horizon will always be at your eye level. Make sure that it is parallel with the top and bottom edge of the paper. Now, from a point in the centre of this horizon, mark your one and only vanishing point. From this point draw five angled lines, two to the left and three to the right of the vanishing point.

∧ **Step 2**
Next, carefully put in six vertical lines that are parallel with the sides of the paper and perpendicular to the horizon, two to the left of the vanishing point and four to the right. These will represent the facades of three large blocks that will appear to stand in the space between the horizon and the foreground.

A Step 3

Finally, you will need to put in six horizontal lines that start from the top and bottom of these verticals, on the left striking off to the left and on the right striking off to the right. Now, when you rub out your guidelines, you will have what appear to be three large blocks set in the space described.

Two-Point Perspective

Two-point perspective uses two vanishing points on the horizon line, and you can use it to show an object or a building from an angle. It is perhaps the most useful type of perspective as it allows you to create a detailed, realistic space.

∧ Step 1

Again, first draw the horizon line across the page, making sure that it is parallel to the top and bottom edges of the paper. Then mark two vanishing points, one on the far left and one on the far right. In the centre draw a shorter vertical line, perpendicular to the horizon and bisecting it, as shown. Now draw lines from the vanishing points to meet the top and bottom of the vertical line at the centre, and extend them across the page, as shown.

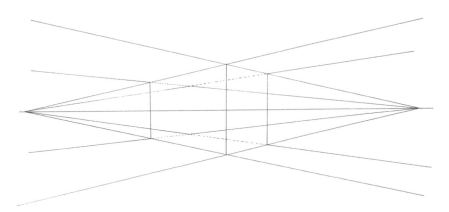

∧ Step 2

To construct the block so that it appears three-dimensional in the scene, you now have to draw two more verticals, parallel to the first, the one to the left further from it than the one to the right. End them both at the lines of perspective, top and bottom, that you have already drawn. Then from the two vanishing points draw two more perspective lines from the left crossing over to meet the top and bottom of the vertical on the right, and from the right to meet the top and bottom of the vertical on the left. This produces a framework for the block apparently set in space.

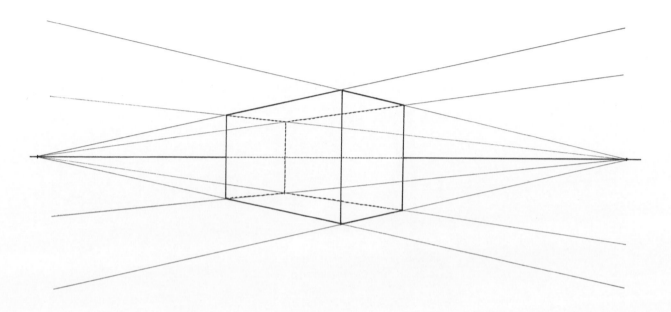

△ **Step 3**

To complete the illusion of a transparent block you will need to draw in the last vertical, which would be hidden if the block were solid. This spans the points where the last sets of perspective lines cross each other. So once again you have drawn an apparently three-dimensional block, but this time transparent.

Three-Point Perspective

Three-point perspective is not often used, but I am demonstrating it here as it helps to complete your understanding of how perspective works. It applies to drawing very tall buildings, and is not so easy to see in real life unless you are standing near the foot of one.

∧ **Step 1**

First, as before, draw a horizon line across the paper and fix two vanishing points to the left and right. Join them to a long vertical drawn in the centre as before at the top and bottom, only the top point should be as far up as you can get on the paper, while the lower point should be close to the eye-level line. This, as you can see, creates a very tall quadrilateral.

∧ **Step 2**

Now draw two lines either side of the central vertical so that they incline equally inwards at the top, as if you had a third vertical vanishing point somewhere high above the horizon – so high above, in fact, that you would need an enormous sheet of paper to accommodate it.

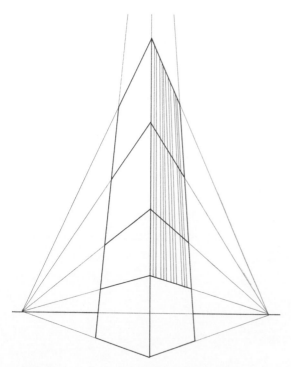

⋀ **Step 3**
Draw in some more lines from the two vanishing points that you can see to indicate different levels on the surface of this tall block, so that it looks like a skyscraper.

⋀ This diagram is more like the form you might actually see, but it would require a massive sheet of paper to actually draw it as a complete diagram.

⋀ **Step 4**
A few more off-vertical lines on one side of the block will increase the drama of the perspective and will give an impression of a tall building, seen from below. Of course, the angularity of the block is vastly exaggerated, but one can get the idea. Remember, perspective is only a way of helping to cheat the eye to believe in the solidity of buildings and the depth of space – it tends to break down if you try to take it too literally.

A Scene in Perspective

Using the techniques of showing perspective that you've just been learning, you are now going to draw an urban scene. You should have largely got the hang of how to construct the drawing of architectural forms so that you can produce a convincing picture, but if you're not satisfied with the end result, don't be discouraged – everything will slot into place with repetition of the basics. This is essentially a perspective exercise, but approached in an artistic rather than scientific way. Your eyes will give you all the information that you need to draw accurately, but your perspective studies will help the mind to make more sense of it and ease the process of drawing. Choose a location that is easy for you to draw and check on the weather before you start to ensure that rain or wind won't make things more difficult for you.

▷ **Step 1**
Here is an outline drawing of a street by the Arno river in Florence, Italy. I haven't included any human figures or cars to make it easier to see the perspective.

Now look at this diagram of the perspective lines that underlie the original drawing, consisting merely of the horizon line and the main lines that join at the vanishing point. These should inform your own drawing, even if you don't actually put them all in with a ruler. So your task is to find a street scene and, if it looks too complex, simplify it by leaving out any street furniture and buildings that confuse you. Draw from life, at the scene, bearing in mind what you now know about perspective construction.

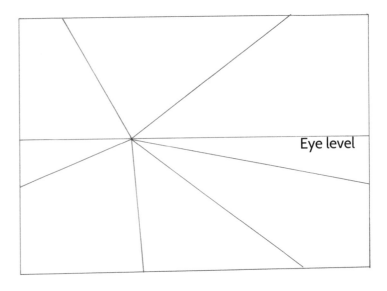

Eye level

▷ Step 2

Put in the main shapes first and the details later, when you are sure that the main blocks of the scene are reasonably convincing.

⋀ Step 3

When you have added all the detail you need, put in the tonal areas, using textures to differentiate the various surfaces of the scene. I have given the roadway a smoother texture than elsewhere by smudging the pencil marks with a stump. Notice also how the more distant features have less definition than those in the foreground, which helps to convince the eye of the picture's three-dimensional quality.

Foreshortening the Human Figure

Here we are concerned with the effects of perspective on the human body when it is seen from an extreme angle. While you may never want to draw someone lying flat out vertically towards you, it will often be the case that you will draw poses where some parts of the figure are closer to you than others, as we saw in the sketches on page 67. So the exercise here is to find someone to lie on the ground or on a couch, as flat as possible, preferably on their back. Your position should be seated so that you can see them from the feet and then the head, from an eye level not far above them.

When you first try this exercise in drawing, the difficulty is in being convinced by the way the legs or head seem to disappear from view, so that there is hardly any length to them in the drawing. It can look unnaturally distorted if you are unused to considering perspective. Nevertheless, your eyes are very good at seeing accurately, and it is only your ideas that make it hard for you to believe what you see. Notice on the male figure how the area covered by the legs and feet is larger than the area of the torso and head, even though we know that, if seen standing up, they would be similar in size.

Also, on the female figure, the head and shoulders seem very big compared to the size of the rest of the body, which recedes from the viewer. It underlines the fact that we perceive objects close to us as larger than those further away. For example, bend your arm, look at your open palm in front of you and watch the size of your hand apparently grow as you bring it towards your nose.

So, when you start to draw your recumbent figure, you may need to draw two lines indicating the way the figure diminishes as it recedes from your viewing point, as I have done in these examples.

When you have blocked in the main forms quite simply, start to draw in the larger shapes, remembering to follow carefully what you observe, not what your mind tells you. Don't be tempted at this stage to put in every small detail; simplicity and accuracy are what you are trying to achieve. Once again, measure how the far parts of the body appear to you in comparison with the nearest parts to ensure that you don't start to enlarge the former or diminish the latter to accord with what you think the human body should look like – many beginners do just this, and it takes a bit of practice before the message sinks in to the mental processes.

Having arrived at a drawing that you are convinced is similar to your view of the figure, proceed to draw in as much detail as you wish, as long as your model is prepared to stay in that position for you. It may mean persuading your model to pose for you on another occasion, but you should draw someone from both the foot and head end. It's an interesting and difficult exercise, but if you didn't find it difficult you wouldn't be learning anything; when things become easier, that's the payoff for the effort you have put in.

An Indoor Scene in Perspective

The final perspective exercise is simpler to stage than the previous ones, because you only have to look around you at the room you are in to see your next subject. That doesn't mean that the task is any easier when it comes to drawing it, but at least you have now had quite a bit of practice of drawing in perspective, so you will be much more confident of tackling the problem.

◁ **Step 1**

First of all, look at this initial sketch of an interior. It will be immediately obvious to you from your studies so far that this scene is using perspective lines to construct the drawing.

∨ **Step 2**

The next diagram shows perspective lines laid over the sketch to help verify my view of the room. You will find that the hardest parts of your own room to see properly are those at the periphery of your vision, in which there is often some slight distortion that would look odd in the drawing. You may have to correct or ignore some of the apparent image at the very edge of your vision.

∧ Step 3

Once you've constructed a sketch that you think holds the image correctly, begin to put in the main outlines of the room and furniture within your field of vision. However, if there are any complicated pieces of furniture or objects that make things more difficult, remove them from view or simply leave them out of your drawing.

All artists learn to adjust the scene in front of them in order to simplify it or make it more interesting and compositionally satisfying; you can see this in the topographical work of Turner, Canaletto or Guardi, for example. The lines of perspective should enable you to get the proportions of the objects in the scene accurate.

Δ Step 4

You can then work on the tonal values of the scene to give it atmosphere and depth. If you have to leave your drawing and come back later, check that the furniture hasn't been moved and that the angle of light is similar to the time before – if the weather is sunny and you try to resume at a different time of day you will potentially find the lights and darks very differently placed. The lighting in my scene is partly from the windows and partly from the overhead electric light. Notice how I have built up the tone to a strong black in the chairs nearest to my viewpoint.

Studying
Still Life

From the exercises this week you will learn about the ways in which you can build up a pleasing still-life composition and gain some practice in the genre. Traditionally the still-life picture was considered the most basic form of composition and one that every artist should know about. It still is the easiest way that an artist can work on his or her skills in any medium, and it's always easily available. Indeed, in your own house you will find numerous still-life arrangements that have occurred without any effort on your part.

As a genre it remains the most accessible way to practise and you should continue to draw still-life subjects throughout your artistic endeavours. No matter how much you draw people, animals or landscapes, the basic drawing of objects remains the simplest way to hone your techniques.

Simple Still Lifes

It isn't difficult to put together a still-life arrangement, but it does require some thought and aesthetic appreciation. If you are a beginner, it's a good idea to accumulate your still-life objects gradually, with some feeling of how the final shape of the arrangement will look. So I began the exercise by simply choosing things that make interesting drawing problems for an artist to solve.

Starting with what happened to be on the top of the plan chest in my studio, I gave myself the challenge of drawing a number of pencils bunched together in a glass jar. I had to find a way of showing the transparency of the pot and the variety of pencil tops poking up out of it – slightly difficult, but not so much so it would become laborious.

Next I took a bowl of oranges that was on my dresser. Fruit in a bowl is a traditional prop for still-life arrangements and presents the challenge of drawing spherical objects that are pushed together by the sides of the bowl.

Both of these subjects are the kind of thing that make a simple still life without any other objects being necessary; of course you might want a bit more background space to show off the quality of your drawing, but nothing else is particularly needed.

Flower in a vase

◁ **Step 1**

I then drew a glass vase with one stalk of flowers in it. This is both simple and complex, because while there is only one flower and one vase, the latter is glass, which can be difficult to draw convincingly, and the flower is a composite stalk of many small blossoms. There are two stages to portraying the subject – first the simple outline of the shape, which you may need to correct a bit, and then the building up of tonal values so that the finished article looks as though it exists in its own space.

Λ **Step 2**

Once you are happy with your outline, make a light tone over all the areas where the shading will be, leaving untouched white paper for the highlights.

◁ **Step 3**

Following this, build up more varied depths of tone to give the objects substance. Note how I have placed the flowers against a dark background to show up their brightness, and the glass vase has a much lighter background in order to make the drawing of the glass simpler. Draw all the distortions that the water and glass produce to give a convincing impression of their quality.

Ephemeral Still Lifes

One of the attractions of still life is the simple, domestic views it often portrays: the tea-tray, a coat thrown over a chair. Even the most simple drawing can catch the feeling of a house or home.

A tea setting is the next arrangement, in its simplest form of just a cup and saucer, teapot and milk jug. This is something you might see in any home at some time.

Now let's look at a rather less decorative still-life composition, a selection of ordinary household tools. The main thing here is to show the power and practicality of the objects as they lie on a surface together. I have purposely not drawn them too smartly, but left them looking a bit rough to emphasize the starkness of the hard-edged tools and the accidental nature of the composition.

Then we see two still-life
arrangements that use the effect of
clothing in the scene: on the right
is a shed door with an old heavy
garment like an overcoat hanging
on a peg. Above is a coat thrown
over a basketwork chair with a pair
of heavy boots on the floor nearby.
They look as if they may be taken
away at any moment.

Here I simply took out the contents of my pockets and put them on the table in front of me. Art students are often given a project like this, in which small objects are drawn magnified to fill out all the space. It's a good exercise that has the effect of encouraging close observation.

Multiple objects such as these melons can be drawn as if laid out for inspection – no special composition, but rather a random pattern of objects.

Composed Arrangements

In contrast to the casual arrangements shown on the previous pages, these examples show a much more formal approach to still-life composition in which each element is carefully arranged to create a work of art.

The next still-life arrangement, drawn after a 19th-century photograph, is very carefully composed to show a selection of food, probably awaiting preparation for a meal. The objects are contrasted with one another, with the smooth eggs in a rounded textured nest while the bigger vegetables are leaning against a handsome ceramic tureen – all combine to make a satisfying composition with aesthetic consideration.

This composition is a very carefully seen, highly simplified arrangement of a mirror on a wall, with a decorative box and a glass cup, all on top of a polished chest of drawers.

A Still-Life Project

Over the next few pages we will consider how you can put together your own still life to create a finished composition. This project might take a few days but I encourage you not to skip the first stages, as every preliminary drawing will help to improve your final piece.

Choosing your subject

The first step is to go around your home and contemplate the different possibilities. I began by walking out into the garden near my studio and, seeing an old watering can, I just started drawing it. It didn't at this stage suggest a composition to me, but it was a good start to the search for objects for the still life.

Back inside my studio, I considered the easel in one corner with a box-easel behind it and a rucksack full of painting kit propped against it – interesting, but not quite varied enough for my taste.

Thinking about a kitchen theme, I got some apples and oranges and laid them out in a way that I might be able to use.

Next, to keep the idea going, I drew a large saucepan and then after that a couple of wine glasses. The theme seemed to be developing.

After that I drew a large box of eggs from the fridge, which provided me with some interesting forms and was a drawing challenge in itself.

All this preliminary work is very useful for working up a good still-life composition. It may take you some time, but it's worth it when you are drawing a major piece of work.

Choosing a composition

Now that my kitchen theme was established, the next stage was to choose my composition pieces and try them out. I roughly scribbled out a simple arrangement of the objects I'd gathered, but I wasn't altogether convinced that it had a future.

So I tried another arrangement but still felt it was not what I really wanted. This scribbling up of various compositions is never wasted, because it helps to clarify what you are really after.

Finally I got something that started to look like the composition that I wanted. All this preparatory work can be done well in advance, but you do have to sit in the position that you think you will be drawing from when it comes to the real thing. Then you quickly start to see what it is that you find attractive.

113

The final composition

∧ Step 1

Now I had a good idea as to what the composition would look like. I carefully arranged all the objects I wanted to see in the drawing, sometimes swapping one object for a similar one in a different size or style. At this stage I drew up the whole composition in a light outline, correcting all the time in order to arrive at a clear cartoon drawing of the whole thing.

∧ Step 2

The next stage was to lay on a single tone that included all the different tones in the drawing, so that I could see exactly how the light was falling on the objects.

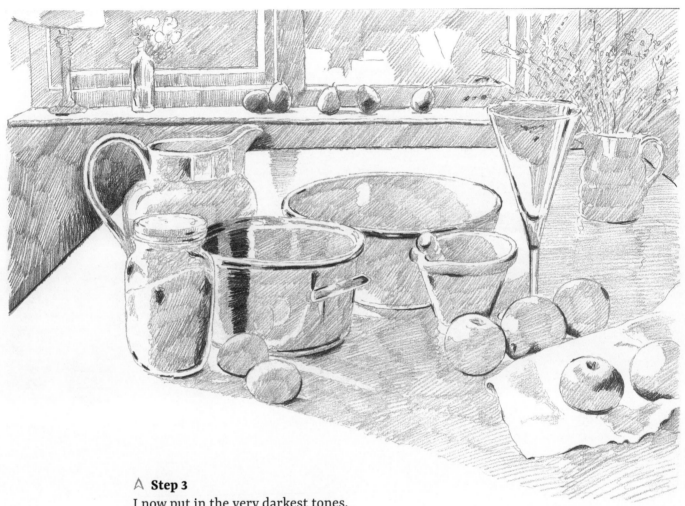

⋀ Step 3

I now put in the very darkest tones, the black areas. This gave me the contrast between the lightest and the darkest tones, and made it much easier to now put in all the mid-tones. This can take some time but if it is done attentively, it will really enhance the quality of the final picture.

∧ Step 4
Finally, the tones between darkest
and lightest can be carefully graded
to build a convincing dimensional
effect, giving the appearance of light
falling across the various objects and
helping to indicate their materiality.

Faces and Portraits

The human face is often the most attractive subject for an artist. In a way, producing a good portrait of another human being proves to yourself how well you are progressing; it's the hardest area in which your skills will be tested, because everyone can see at once whether you have attained a resemblance to the individual or not.

However, that isn't the be all and end all of a portrait – it's also meant to be a work of art, not just an accurate record of someone's features. In this lesson you'll learn about drawing portraits in a way that will enable you to capture likenesses of your friends and family as well as producing pictures that stand up as art in their own right.

Arranging the setting for a portrait requires some thought – you will need to consider not just the character of the sitter but also the way in which they are lit and posed. This can give vastly different effects to the style of the portrait and make it much more interesting, both for the sitter and the artist. Some portraits are of the formal and serious kind, such as an institution might commission for posterity, while others are informal and domestic, often of people that we know quite well. The sitter may be against a blank background that tells nothing of their lifestyle, or there may be details of their surroundings, perhaps with symbolic meanings. It's a field of art that has many fascinating variations.

Portrait Composition

The first thing to consider in a portrait is the format to choose, which will be largely dictated by how much of the sitter and the background we wish to show. Here, we look at the choices made by various artists to convey different effects in their portraits.

Celia Bennett's is the kind of portrait that shows only the head of the sitter, as large as possible in the frame, with a dead straight, full-face view. This style is probably what most people first think of when it comes to drawing a portrait, and it is a good way for you to start because it is a very basic version.

In the next picture, after Lucie Cookson, you can see the upper torso and the arms of the sitter, and the head is turned to one side with the eyes directed away from the artist. This has the effect of making the portrait a little less head on, and allows the artist to give some sense of the sitter's body language. Note the rather interesting lighting as well.

In this head and shoulders portrait after Keith Robinson, the sitter's head is slightly turned and lowered. The space around the head also gives a more formal effect to the portrait, but the whole look is very gentle and attractive.

This drawing after a portrait by Geert Schless also shows the head and shoulders, but in profile, which immediately gives a more formal and less emotionally connected effect as if the artist is making a cool study of the head. People who commission portraits don't tend to ask for this view because it is not how they usually see themselves. It is very objective in style, but was quite popular during the Renaissance period in Italy.

The next sitter is posed in the frame of a large window that reflects the electric light in its dark panes. He is portrayed very formally by Oisin Roche, almost like a royal portrait. He takes up only a relatively small proportion of the space, the window becoming a large part of the scene. This could be considered as a half-figure portrait, but the forcefulness of the pose makes us somehow aware of the complete person.

Now we see a full-length portrait of a seated woman, after the artist Toby Wiggins. Although the sitter looks quite gentle and relaxed, because she is surrounded by space and the dark shadow of that space throws the figure forward, the effect is much more powerful and dramatic.

Sara Shamma's female figure is displayed like an exotic flower, her hand holding up a smoking cigarillo, with a jewelled pendant suspended in front of her. Her shadow cast on the background wall is complex and her hand is drawn several times as if the artist couldn't quite decide which was the best position. She also wears decorative clothing, and the whole effect is of this exquisite creature posing for our delight – an interesting statement by the artist of herself as a sort of odalisque.

Drawing two or more people introduces a new dynamic into a portrait since you have to consider how the figures interact: whether they will be in physical contact, and whether they will be looking at each other or at the viewer, as well as where they are placed in the frame.

Professors Chris and Uta Frith, after artist Emma Wesley, is of a husband and wife sitting in their own study. The scene is full of what are probably connections with their own interests and academic work. They are closely placed together, but are looking at us sideways, as though we have just come into the room. It is both formal and friendly, which is quite a difficult thing to achieve, and shows the artist's powers.

Drawing Your Family

Now let's look at what happens when we choose our nearest and dearest for our portrait sitters. Most of us have enough family and friends to practise our drawing skills on, and it is of great benefit to draw the people you have easiest access to and whom you know very well. This in-depth knowledge can help to give your portraits more power.

I decided to have a go at drawing most of the members of my family who were in the house one Christmas, and I started with my grandchildren. Of course young children and babies will not sit still for you much so this is probably an occasion when photography can come to your aid. It does help to have the originals around as well, though, because this helps to inform your drawings from photographs that you have taken yourself.

Here is my youngest grandson, caught in his mother's arms and laughing at the camera. As you can see, his round, open eyes and nose and mouth are all set neatly in the centre of the rounded form of his head and face.

Next my granddaughter lounging on the floor, kicking her legs and giggling. Here, I concentrated on her gleeful expression.

121

I drew my youngest daughter while she was talking to someone else, so almost unaware of me.

Then come drawings of my wife and my youngest son's girlfriend, both engaged in conversation with other people. Catching a fleeting expression is not easy, but with a little practice, you soon get it right.

My eldest grandson, looking a bit shy but amused. He couldn't stay still for long, so I took a photograph just before I started drawing.

Next my son-in-law grinning at the camera (left) and my youngest son about to go out (below). My son's hat helped to define the facial area rather neatly and give character to the drawing.

All these drawings of my family were done close together in time, often based on photographs that I took myself and informed by the people being close by at the time. It is an enjoyable and instructive exercise that is well worth doing.

A Portrait Project

This exercise entails quite a bit of drawing and you will learn a lot about your model's appearance by spending a whole session drawing and redrawing him or her from as many different angles as you think would be useful.

Sketches of the head

I chose as my sitter my eldest daughter, who has sat for me often, like all of my family. Not only that, she is an accomplished artist herself, so she knows the problems of drawing from life. This sympathy with your endeavours is useful, as models do get bored with sitting still for too long.

I worked my way round my sitter's head by drawing her first from the side or profile view, then from a more three-quarters view and finally full face. I now had a good idea as to the physiognomy of her face.

Sketching different poses

Now you need to spend some time drawing the sitter full or three-quarter length in order to decide how much of the figure you might want to draw.

First I drew my daughter standing, with her arm draped across a mantelpiece, which gave me a three-quarter figure.

Next I tried a side view of her kneeling on the rug, which made quite a nice compact shape.

Then I asked her to sit in a big easy chair with her legs crossed. Notice how she is looking out of the picture.

Another variation on a seated pose came next. Notice how all these drawings are much less detailed than the face drawings, because here I was just looking for a pose and I wasn't worried about whether the face was accurate; the position was everything.

Drawing the features in detail

Once you've decided upon the pose you need to turn your attention to the details of the sitter's face, taking each of the features and making detailed drawings of them.

I started by drawing just one eye. This is a difficult thing to do, as the model will find your concentrated stare a little daunting. However, it's also very revealing as to how carefully you have observed the eye. Having drawn my daughter's eye directly facing me, I then drew it from a slight angle so that I got a side view of it. I did this with both eyes, then drew them as a pair to see how they looked together, as well as the space between them.

Next I moved on to the mouth and drew it two or three times, exploring the front, side and three-quarter views.

Following that I drew the nose, first in profile, then from the front and also with the eyes and mouth to get an idea of how they looked in relation to each other.

As my model had quite long hair hiding her ears, I didn't draw the latter but went straight on to drawing the hair from several angles, one of which would probably appear in the final portrait.

I now had drawings of the head, the pose and all the features, so I was well set up to begin my portrait.

127

The final composition

 Step 1
With my drawings gathered together and my model refreshed and ready to sit for me again, I first drew up a quick sketch that told me where everything would be placed. I had decided to position her on a large sofa, legs stretched out and hands in her lap, with her head slightly turned to look directly at me.

▷ **Step 2**
Then, using my sketch as a guide, I drew up a careful outline drawing of the whole figure and the background setting in some detail. This was the last stage at which I could introduce any changes if they were necessary.

∧ **Step 3**
Next I began to put in the main area of
tone evenly, using the lightest tone that
would appear on the finished article.
The light was all derived from the large
window to the left and so half of my
daughter's face was in soft shadow.

∧ Step 4

I could now build up all the different tones until I had produced a convincing three-dimensional portrait that looked like my sitter. This may have struck you as quite a long process, but if you take all this trouble to make your own portrait the chances are that not only will the sitter be pleased with the result, so will you.

Exploring Landscapes

In this final week of the course, we return to the subject of landscapes, which you started in Week 4. I've made landscape the last topic to explore in detail because it's probably the area for which you will need the most preparation. One habit that will help you is to always take a small sketchbook when you are out and about so that you can make a quick record of any appealing locations for later reference. Another useful tool is your camera, because when you take shots of landscapes you can bear in mind how you might want to draw the scene, which has a way of sharpening your compositional skills.

Sometimes you will find you need to alter the landscape to a certain extent when you are drawing, which is a time-honoured practice of artists working in both the rural and urban landscape. However, it's best at first to concentrate on getting the landscape you are drawing as accurate as possible, and then contribute your own ideas to the scene later on when you are more confident.

You will spend more time on a landscape than on any of the other subjects in this book because the sheer scale of a location demands more work and effort. However, when you have finished one you will find it extremely rewarding to have a record of where you have been. There is also something in the human soul that responds to scenes of the natural world; it's no accident that most pictures that you see on living-room walls tend to be landscapes of some sort.

Looking for Variety

The idea of drawing a landscape can be a bit daunting at first because of the sheer size of the view and the amount of information therein. However, it is not quite so difficult as it looks at first glance and you'll soon gain confidence with a little practice. Trying the drawings shown here will give you a good start.

The first is of a hilltop farmhouse in Tuscany, Italy. The scene is nicely set, with no confusing background to perplex you, and you need only draw the slope of the hill, a few trees and the shape of the farmhouse. This sort of carefully limited view is ideal for a first attempt because it doesn't create the problem of having to decide which part of the view to choose; there is only one major building that is anywhere near to the artist's viewpoint. Another advantage is that there is little or no perspective to wrestle with.

This view of Polperro in Cornwall, seen from above the harbour, is a little more difficult. Once again it is a restricted view so that you can see only a certain amount of the town, but even so there are more houses, or at least rooftops, to draw. I have concentrated on the main part of the harbour and the trees just above it; the only houses that I have drawn in any detail are those directly in the centre. The background and the mass of roofs on the left are just shown in a sort of inspired scribble to suggest the general shape and feel.

This view of the Houses of Parliament, Big Ben and Westminster Bridge in London is famous worldwide. Drawing a familiar scene such as this is a challenge, because a certain amount of accuracy is required. The whole scene composes itself to some degree, your choice being only how much to extend the scene to the right or left of the focal point of the clock tower. The bridge is a problem in perspective, but as long as you don't try to get too much of it in the picture it's not too difficult. The hardest job here is the intricacy of the architecture of the main buildings, but keep them simple to start with as I have done here.

Here I have drawn the viaduct bridge over the River Wear in Devon, which combines awe-inspiring architecture with beautiful countryside. This sort of landscape is dramatic from many angles, but I have chosen the most obvious to show the shape of the bridge and its reflection in the river. It also helps that the sun is behind the bridge, making it into a marvellous silhouette against the bright sky and stream.

This view across the formal gardens of Hampton Court Palace just outside London is a study in gardening on a grand scale. The whole scene is a carefully composed pattern of plants and paths, with the mass of the building in the background nicely balancing the soft formality of the lawns and flowers in the foreground. Only part of the garden is shown, which stops it becoming too panoramic – what you might call a domesticated environment, but on a grand scale.

This grand panorama of Dartmoor, in Devon, is by the Victorian artist John William Inchbold. With this type of landscape you need to find a place that gives you key features to help frame the composition, which Inchbold has done well with the large rock on the left and the deep ravine on the right. The sweep of the sky is kept to about one-quarter of the whole area of the picture, so that it doesn't distract from the rugged scenery. Overall accuracy is not the most important part of a drawing such as this – capturing the atmosphere of the place comes first.

Leading the Eye into the Picture

In the examples shown here a path or waterway draws the eye into the scene by leading away from the foreground into the distance. This very effective device is often used by artists to add interest to the picture.

In this view of the Chianti countryside in Italy a path winds across the scene past the open vineyards and a farm, disappearing into the hills. Nearly all the main features are on the right side of the picture, but they create a horizontal thrust across the scene, counter to the direction of the path.

The next scene is from Venice, Italy – a canal on the island of Burano with boats cluttering the edges of the water and a church tower looming up in the distance. Once again we appear to be looking along the canal and the row of houses alongside it.

Enclosed Spaces

This example is of an urban landscape which is very circumscribed by the setting. It shows a William Ratcliffe painting of Clarence Gardens in north London, dated 1912. Townscapes like this are useful for the artist because the enclosed space makes it simpler to choose your viewing point and how much to draw. The angle of the daylight will also help you to decide your viewpoint – you can choose whether you want to draw with the light from the side, from behind, or against you as in the example below.

Elements of Landscape

Water

Water in a landscape always adds an extra dimension to a drawing, reflecting the sky and the scenery and bringing light into your work. You may be lucky enough to live near the sea, but a river or lake will be just as interesting for studies of water.

In this scene the water is in rapid movement and so does not reflect the landscape and sky as much as just the light. The surrounding scenery is the side of a rocky hill and the stream flows down to a pool at the base of the picture. There is not much sky as the depth of the hillside needs to be shown, and there is little vegetation except for grass. It is in effect a portrait of a waterfall. Most of the water is the white of the paper, and to make it work the rest of the picture needs some pencil work to provide contrast.

The next picture is of the Suffolk coast, along a creek where fishing boats are moored. In the forefront of the scene are a couple of boats tied to a jetty, with the water behind and in the distance the other shore, also with moored boats. The sky is clear and the water reflects that light, with only small ripples of reflection shown where the boats are. The weather is calm and still, so there is almost nothing to see in the sky and the water.

Trees

The next exercise is to make a study of trees, because they are present in most landscapes. Your earlier go at trees in Week 4 (see page 50) will have given you the basics, but now the task is to concentrate in more detail on two or three species – choose ones that grow close to where you live so that you can easily revisit them. Shown here are the works of two artists from the 19th century to give you some idea of the power and strength of skilfully drawn trees.

The first artist is Samuel Palmer, who portrayed the landscapes of south-east England. His drawing here of oak and beech trees in the woods is a magnificent example of the stature that the trunk of a large tree can give to a picture, if drawn expressively. This is an exercise that you could emulate and learn a lot about drawing in the process.

The second artist is John Constable, drawing in the Vale of Dedham in Suffolk. His beautifully realized clump of trees, with their intertwining branches and masses of leafy texture contrasting the hardness of the wood, is a lesson in itself. Copy a Constable drawing of a tree to discover some of his methods, then have a go at drawing leaves in a similar fashion.

Plants

While plants can be loosely indicated in the larger landscape you will sometimes want to draw them in more detail, perhaps in the foreground to add a sense of depth to a panoramic picture or in a more intimate, small-scale study.

This view of a valley with a tower and other buildings is seen past the profusion of wild plants on the side of the hillside nearest to our viewpoint. The nearer plants are drawn more heavily in outline than the buildings in the background, which helps to bring the foreground plants forward and push the buildings back.

This edge of a countryside path has the usual mix of wild plants growing along it – a good test of your drawing ability, even if they never end up in a complete landscape.

A Landscape Project

The first step towards drawing a landscape is deciding on a location. I am lucky to live near the beautiful Richmond Park in London, so I went on a long walk there with my sketchbook, stopping every now and then to draw what I saw in front of me.

Sketching on location

The first pause was to draw this view of one of the lakes seen through some large trees. As it was winter there wasn't much foliage, but the bare branches of the taller trees were very attractive things to draw.

Then I moved on to a more open area where a hillside swept up to some woods in the distance. I quickly made a sketch of this.

I then drew another glimpse of the lake from a distance, without any trees in front of it. This might come in handy for a background feature.

I noticed in the distance a small group of the deer that live in this park and sketched them. It wasn't possible to get very close to them, but they could well be a focal point in a final picture.

I then moved down the hill towards a stream, drawing an attractive tree on the way and then part of a reflection in the stream. I didn't take this very far, because I was realizing that I had now decided what and where I was going to draw.

On top of a hill I drew another log, a man resting on the ground, and a wooden bench. Nearby was a marvellous old dead tree trunk, split and twisted, making a beautiful sculptural shape, that might be a feature for a foreground.

141

The final composition

⊳ Step 1

My proposed landscape was to be a view up a hillside, with a large dead tree trunk lying across the path in the foreground. I also thought a couple of deer could appear somewhere in the picture – that is to say, my landscape would be a composite of several views. I made a rough sketch to see how it might look.

⊲ Step 2

Feeling that it would work well, I proceeded to draw it up in line only, at which point I could sort out any difficulties of composition and drawing.

⊳ Step 3

Once I had made all the corrections I needed to I could now begin to put in the texture and tone to give the picture more body. At this stage I kept the tone even and at its lightest, just in case I needed to change anything.

∀ **Step 4**

Then came the final push to build up the depth and feeling of space that I wanted to see in the drawing. The deer almost disappear on the hillside, but they do work as a muted focal point in the composition. The path going up the hill helps to draw the eye into the picture and the undulating horizon of the hillside draws the eye around the picture to the dead tree standing on the left.

The whole project does require a certain amount of patience and determination, since drawing landscapes can be very time-consuming; when I go out to embark upon a landscape I always allow the best part of a day to do it. But of course once you become absorbed in drawing you will find yourself spending longer and longer drawing the subjects you like. You should by all means go along with this until you feel you have achieved at least some expertise. However, do make

an effort then to try something that has not inspired you so far, and you may discover that honing your skill in one area has suddenly made another more appealing.

Indeed, an artist can find interest in everything, which is why I find drawing such a rewarding subject to master. So good luck in all your efforts, and I hope this course goes some way towards helping you achieve what you want to in the world of art.

Index